THE
WILDING
WAY

Apple Sauce

The Wilding family's coat of arms
includes an apple tree. The *Oxford
English Dictionary* gives, among others,
the following meanings of 'wilding':

1525 – a wild apple or apple-tree
1577 – a wild plant, flower or fruit
1697 – *(chiefly poetic)* growing wild

1 'Official' fan club photo

2 Dancing with Anna in *Spring in Park Lane*

THE WILDING WAY

the story of my life
by Michael Wilding

ST. MARTIN'S PRESS
NEW YORK

THE WILDING WAY. Copyright © 1982 by Pamela Wilcox and
the Estate of Michael Wilding. All rights reserved.
Printed in the United States of America. No part of this book
may be used or reproduced in any manner whatsoever without
written permission except in the case of brief quotations
embodied in critical articles or reviews. For information,
address St. Martin's Press, 175 Fifth Avenue,
New York, N.Y. 10010.

Library of Congress Cataloging in Publication Data

Wilding, Michael, 1912-1979.
  The Wilding way.

  British ed. published under title: Apple sauce.
  Includes index.
  1. Wilding, Michael, 1912-1979. 2. Moving-picture
actors and actresses—Great Britain—Biography.
I. Wilcox, Pamela. II. Title.
PN2598.W48A38 1982 791.43′028′0924 [B]   82-10754
ISBN 0-321-87954-7

First published in Great Britain under the title *Apple Sauce*
by George Allen & Unwin Ltd.

First U.S. Edition

10 9 8 7 6 5 4 3 2 1

Dedicated
in fond and grateful memory to
Herbert Wilcox
who made me a star.

Acknowledgments

Many people have helped in preparing this book for publication—by checking facts, dates and recollections, reading and commenting on the typescript and in many other ways – but special thanks are due to Dr L. J. Beynon, Dirk Bogarde, Sir John Clements, Lionel Crane, Brenda Davies, Brian Eagles, Sir John Gielgud, Lord Peter Graves, Miriam Hodgson, Wendy Jordan, Peter Leek, Margaret Lockwood, Sam Marx, Jack Middleton, Dame Ann Neagle, June Peskett and Kelly, Patricia Perilli of the British Film Institute (for her help with the film list), Jean Riley, Geoffrey Smith, Diana Tyler and Michael Trubshawe.

Grateful thanks are also due to the Estate of Michael Wilding, EMI Films Ltd, Metro-Goldwyn-Mayer, Inc, Rank Film Distributors, Twentieth Century-Fox Film Co Ltd, Leon A. Gutman, Inc, John and Charmaine Ball, the British Film Institute, the *Daily Express* and the Solent News Agency for supplying or giving permission to reproduce stills and photographs; and to Wardville Productions Ltd for permission to quote from Dame Anna Neagle's autobiography *There's Always Tomorrow* (published by W. H. Allen in 1974 and in paperback by Futura in 1979) and to Everest Pictures Ltd for permission to quote from Herbert Wilcox's autobiography *Twenty-Five Thousand Sunsets* (published by Bodley Head in 1967).

I am indebted too to Dick Sheppard, whose book *Elizabeth* (published by W. H. Allen in 1975) has been a useful source of reference, as has been *Marlene* by Charles Higham (published by Hart Davis in 1978 and in paperback by Mayflower in 1979).

Pamela Wilcox

Contents

List of Illustrations

xii *The Wilding Way*

Prologue
by Pamela Wilcox

THIS is the story of a man who became the number one idol of the post-war British cinema. Emerging from the ruins of the blitz, Britain was ill housed, ill fed and filled with disenchantment about a peace so bitterly won. Rationing and austerity were still the order of the day, turning sour even the taste of victory. In such an era, the witty, handsome figure of Michael Wilding, in partnership with Anna Neagle and under the direction of my father, Herbert Wilcox, brought to jaded British cinema audiences, romance, escape and a hint of a more hopeful future.

In 1948, after Wilding had been voted Britain's most popular film star for the third year in succession, Wilcox decided to widen his star rating and loaned him to Alfred Hitchcock, who cast him in two successful films, first with Ingrid Bergman then with Marlene Dietrich. As a result, Wilding won international acclaim. Writing at the time in the *Daily Graphic*, the film critic Elspeth Grant summed up the essence of his popularity: 'Michael Wilding has proved himself to be of that very rare species, a truly romantic British male. None can match him for wit, charm and sheer dazzlement of personality.'

What made Wilding so unmatchable among his contemporaries? Trevor Howard was certainly a name to reckon with. Top of the film polls as a result of the highly successful *Wicked Lady* was James Mason, whose forte was the sombre, even sinister role. Then there was the tight-lipped John Clements, who had a habit of dying in the fade-out. John Mills was probably everyone's idea of a typical Englishman, whether he spoke with a Cockney accent or a stiff upper lip. Stewart Granger could be considered Wilding's closest rival as a heart-throb, but he was cast mostly in costume pictures. None of these stars could master what Wilding appeared to accomplish so effortlessly – the combination of romance and humour.

A news columnist recently called Wilding 'the Robert Redford of the fifties'. However, Reg Whitley perhaps came nearer the mark when he wrote 'Michael Wilding is Britain's answer to Cary Grant' and Caroline Lejeune probably summed up his qualities best of all when she wrote in the *Sunday Times* 'Wilding is the King of romantic comedy. His only real rival is David Niven. But Niven was discovered and nurtured in Hollywood, whereas Wilding remains a totally British discovery.'

So much for the qualities that made Wilding a star. What about his character as a man? He had one outstanding trait, which even in his sixties he still possessed in plenty – his attraction to and for the opposite sex. His old-time friend and fellow actor Peter Graves put it succinctly: 'I could never get over the looks of any of Michael's ladies. He's been surrounded by dazzlingly beautiful, talented women all his life.'

It is, therefore, all the more surprising to discover that he lacked any trace of vanity. This was as true at the time of his death as it was when I first met him over twenty-five years ago. For instance, he wouldn't even take his share of the credit for the outstanding good looks of both his sons by Elizabeth Taylor. He just shrugged his shoulders and said 'What do you expect with such a beautiful mother?' Yet three of the most beautiful women in the world fell in love with him and two of them married him.

The facet of his personality which struck me most forcibly as we worked together on this book was his persistent and often infuriating modesty. Indeed, one theme that emerges from these pages is the contradiction between Michael's own negative view of his achievements and the contrasting opinions of the people who worked with him – including, among many others, Alfred Hitchcock, Noel Coward, John Gielgud, Terence Rattigan, Marlene Dietrich, Dame Anna Neagle and my father.

When we first discussed this book, I told Michael bluntly that he would have to be completely frank about every aspect of his life and career. So, for the first time, he tells the history of an ailment which dogged both his career and private life since his teens. He told me that in so doing he hoped he might give some hope and encouragement to those similarly afflicted. With his usual simplicity he declared 'I shall abide by Cromwell's instructions to his portrait painter: "Paint me plain. Warts and all."'

1

What Ho, She Bumps!

O NE of my earliest memories is of a beautiful summer's day in Moscow. My parents had taken me on a swimming expedition to a long, thin lake south of the city, with our Norwegian nanny, Norgan. When we reached the lake, my mother turned to me and said 'Now, darling, take all your clothes off.' 'I can't do that!' I protested, feeling a blush run up my cheeks. My mother burst out laughing. 'Now then,' she said reassuringly, 'there's nothing to be shy about. Norgan sees you every day without your clothes when she gives you your bath.' But somehow this didn't seem the same thing at all. 'Go on,' urged my mother, 'your father is waiting for you in the lake.' Red-faced with embarrassment, I did as I was told, but not before I had turned my back on Norgan and my mother and sought shelter behind a bush. Stark naked, I stayed behind the bush until I heard my father's voice – 'Come out from behind that bush and let's see if we can make a water baby out of you!' With my hands covering my private parts, I made a rush for the water's edge. 'Come on in and climb on my back,' said father.

I found it quite pleasant sailing along on his back, while he did a gentle breast-stroke. Suddenly I noticed that all the swimmers at our end of the lake were men and boys – and that they were all completely naked. Then I saw something else – something very strange. At the other end of the lake ladies were splashing about. They too were stark naked and I could see at once, even at that distance, that their chests were different from ours. They had bumps on them.

This, my first sight of the naked female form, made a deep impression on me and I thought about the bumps long after we got home. In fact I dreamed about them that night. My curiosity could not be contained, so next morning I went down to the kitchen where our cook Lucia was working. I explained to her about the lake and how the gentlemen bathed at one end and the ladies at the other. Then, with the perfect manners instilled into me by my parents, I bowed and said 'Please Lucia, will you take off your blouse so I can see your bumps?' Lucia smiled and graciously complied. After a long look, I bowed again, one hand on my tummy and the other behind my back, and thanked her profoundly. I thank her to this day.

I hasten to add that nothing untoward had occurred during my early childhood to arouse in me such a precocious interest in the female form. I was born at Leigh-on-Sea on 23 July 1912 and christened Michael Charles Gauntlet Wilding. My father told me I was a direct descendant of the archbishop of Canterbury who had crowned Queen Victoria. Also, that I was an indirect descendant of John of Gaunt, hence my third name.

My father told me more about my family's somewhat questionable history. One of my forebears, while on a country walk in Shropshire, from where the Wildings hail, stopped at a local inn to refresh himself. Looking around for something to read, he spied an ancient, battered copy of *The Landed Gentry*. When he reached the letter 'W' he received something of a shock. The entry under the name Wilding ran to just one line and read 'The Wildings are a drunken godless lot.'

My family also had connections with Russia that went back several generations. I first learned this while at school in England when the headmaster had me on the carpet for beating the living daylights out of a notorious teenage bully. When I got home that night my father came straight to the point: 'I have had a call from your headmaster. Why did you beat up that boy?' 'Because he was a bully,' I replied, 'and he got on my wick.' To my surprise my father grinned and patted me on the back. 'Well done,' he said, 'but watch that temper of yours. You see, Michael, you have a drop of wild Russian blood. Not much. Just a drop.' Years later I found out that in the middle of the eighteenth century a member of our family had married the daughter of the Chancellor to the Empress of all the Russias.

My grandfather served in the Russian Diplomatic Corps until he retired and returned to England with his wife to live in a very pretty house in Kidlington. I must have been about eight when I was first introduced to this charming old couple. My grandmother, who bore an uncanny resemblance to Queen Mary, invited us over to lunch. After the meal was over, I bowed low and kissed my grandmother's hand. She hugged me, saying 'What an elegant little gentleman I have as a grandson!' I still think good manners are important and try to live up to my father's guiding motto, 'Manners makyth man'.

Although I loved my father deeply, as a child I was much impressed by his many achievements and his strict code of morals. Henry Wilding, MBE, was born in Petrograd and educated at King's School, Canterbury, said at the time to be academically second only to Eton. There he became a brilliant scholar, excelling in Latin and Greek. After university he joined the Army, served in Africa and was twice recommended for the Military Cross. It was not until after his death that I discovered a large gold star attached to a ribbon. This was awarded for extreme bravery in service with the White Russian Army during the Revolution and was said also to bestow honour on the recipient's entire family.

But my father was not given to talking about his exploits and not until I was grown up did I discover how bravery, not only in the field of battle but also against almost constant illness, had shaped his life. He contracted malaria in Africa and was invalided home. The disease persisted on and off for two years, and at the end of that time, rather than re-enter the Army with a lower rank, he went into business in the City, which he hated, but which offered the only immediate alternative means of earning a living.

About this time he met a beautiful Scots girl, Ethel Thomas. Although they never admitted it, I have a hunch that my father picked up my mother on a train journey. Judging by the photographs of her as a young girl, who could blame him? When they were first married they went to live in Roehampton. They both desperately wanted children and after three years had passed without their wish being granted my mother told my father that she had consulted the family doctor, who advised a move to the seaside. My father plumped for Leigh-on-Sea, which was near enough to London for him to travel to his office.

Sure enough, within a year my elder brother Alistair was born and I followed two years later. My mother was forty-two when I was born and after the birth she had difficulty in walking and became a semi-invalid for a time. When I was old enough to understand, I used to blame myself for her ill-health and was filled with guilt.

If my feelings for my father were based chiefly on respect, my devotion to my mother knew no bounds. I just adored her. We always seemed to be on the same wavelength. Her father had died when she was three but she thought the world of her stepfather, who in turn recognised her exceptional talents. She could sing like a bird and had the most strikingly tender and evocative speaking voice. She had studied piano and elocution at the Royal Academy of Music. One day the principal told her, 'You should make use of your beautiful voice and go on the stage.' 'The stage!' she cried, 'surely that is rather an improper calling?'

Nevertheless, on the stage she went. Here our careers ran parallel, for in a sense we both started out with one foot already on the ladder of success. My mother made her

début as an actress not in the wilds of Coventry or
Northampton but in the heart of the West End. True she
only played a small part in a 'curtain-raiser' at the
Lyceum, but that was enough to get her photograph on
the front page of the *Tatler*. She showed me the picture
with a mixture of pleasure and astonishment. 'You see,'
she explained, 'in those days the *Tatler*'s front page,
indeed all its pages, were usually reserved for society debs
or lords and ladies.'

Following this promising début she went on tour for a
year with a distinguished theatrical company headed by
the leading actor of the day, Sir Ben Greet. She told me
proudly in later years 'I was leading lady in Sir Ben Greet's
company when a young girl called Sybil Thorndike was
just a "walk-on".' There was no doubt that a brilliant
stage career awaited her. Then she met my father and, as
she put it to me when I was old enough to understand, 'I
gave up the stage to become a wife and mother and I have
never had a moment's regret.'

When she died at the age of seventy-six, I was 6,000
miles away filming in Hollywood. The studio refused me
leave to return for her funeral because my absence would
have meant delayed production. Strange as it may sound, I
felt a certain sense of relief. She was cremated at Golders
Green and I did not think I could have gone through such
grim proceedings without breaking down utterly. I
preferred to keep my last memory of her as a gay, wise
woman, who had done more than anyone else in shaping
my life. Whatever good qualities survive in my somewhat
ambiguous character I owe entirely to her influence.

Just after I had celebrated my third birthday my father
was recalled to Moscow to serve with military intelligence.
To a devoted family man separation from his wife and
young brood was unthinkable, so Alistair and I were
destined to spend our formative years in a strange city and
unknown land.

My two years in Moscow passed happily enough. I
lorded it at ritzy children's parties and because I could

speak both English and Russian was always in great demand. On one occasion a fashionable Moscow baroness gave me a seat of honour next to her at the head of the table with the request that I should tip her off if I noticed any of the young guests misbehaving. The party was in full swing when I glanced down to the end of the table and spotted a tot of about three turning green at the gills under a smudge of strawberry jam. Promptly, I tapped my hostess on the shoulder. 'Excuse me,' I said, 'but I think Prince Boris is going to throw up!'

Young though I was, I was aware that Russia was a country over which the landowners ruled while the majority worked as slaves. One incident during a train journey summed up the difference between the privileged few and the penniless many. Sharing our carriage was a nobleman swathed in furs. He had just finished consuming the contents of a large picnic basket when the train came to a halt. Outside the window I saw a long line of peasants, their backs bent, tilling the soil. Suddenly, the nobleman opened the carriage window and emptied the remains of his meal on to the track. There was a sudden shout from the peasants. Then like wild animals they scrambled up the embankment and fought and tussled with one another over the scraps.

When my name first appeared in the newspapers as an up-and-coming film star, the drama of my childhood exodus from Russia was often exaggerated. I was expected to tell tales of the 'wicked Reds' and discourse on the evils of Communism. In reality, our departure could hardly have been less dramatic. Naturally, my father's position as diplomatic attaché to the White Army was now obsolete. If we had stayed on through the thick of the 1917 Revolution we might have been in danger. My father acted quietly but swiftly. I do not recall any sense of panic surrounding our departure, although as we drove to the station I could see barricades and machine-guns lining the streets.

2
Blue-Coat Boy

WHEN we reached England, my father found he had lost touch with his old financial contacts, and I sensed his air of harassment. After all, he was not a born businessman. There was now no chance of my going to King's, Canterbury. Finally, after much thought, he decided to send me as a boarder to Christ's Hospital school, which charged no fees or a sum according to one's means.

There was no entrance exam worth speaking of. If you could spell 'cat' or 'dog' and hadn't got VD you were in. Christ's provided a broad education in the best sense of the word, inasmuch as there was no snobbery. I found myself fascinated by the variety of accents and here began my flair for mimicry.

While I felt a certain pride in belonging to a school whose traditions went back to the reign of Edward VI, I hated the archaic uniform we were forced to wear – long yellow stockings, topped by a dark blue coat tied round the waist with a girdle, which gave us our name – blue-coat boys. Once every year we were marched in crocodile from Waterloo Station to the Mansion House where we were each given a newly minted sixpence. Girls would lean out of office windows and whistle and cheer, making us feel as if we were part of a circus. Once at the Mansion House, we accepted the money like grateful angels. But the return journey meant catching a train at East Croydon and in the absence of any masters we behaved like a bunch of hooligans. On the station the air was thick with barrages of buns and orange peel hurled at innocent passengers. Indeed, one such journey provoked what might be called my first public appearance.

As the train pulled out of the station, much to the consternation of our fellow passengers, an equally boisterous companion and I were hanging our heads out of the window howling war-whoops. Suddenly I spotted a sort of lever. My companion dared me to give it a twist. Naturally I accepted the dare; but when I got back to my seat I noticed with horror that the communication cord was hanging loose. The train ground to a shuddering halt. A few minutes later the guard burst into our carriage full of rage. 'Come on now. I know you've been up to your tricks again. Own up. Who did it?' 'Not me,' I lied putting on an angelic face. 'Not us,' chorused the rest of the lads. But the guard was not fooled. 'Your headmaster is going to hear about this,' he said grimly. 'Don't think you can go about stopping trains and get away with it.'

Sure enough, at the beginning of morning assembly the following day the headmaster named the four of us who had been in the carriage and told us to stand up. 'Now then,' he demanded, 'which one of you pulled that communication cord?' Complete silence from all four of us. 'Either the culprit owns up or all four of you will get a beating,' he warned. There was nothing else for it. 'It was me, sir,' I admitted. 'But I dared him,' chimed in my loyal companion. The two of us got a well deserved beating at the hands of the headmaster. Being beaten at Christ's was no new experience for me, although my experience there was exceptional. For no reason that I could ever fathom one of the masters had taken an instant dislike to me. On my first day, he singled me out of the rest of the class. 'Stand up, Wilding,' he said. I stood up. 'Take your pants down and come over here,' he commanded and proceeded to give me a thorough beating in front of the whole class – the first of many.

My academic progress was unremarkable apart from the fact that I had discovered myself to be an expert mimic. I could even imitate physical attributes. Although I had no natural bent for sports, by watching and copying the actions of a good swimmer or a fine batsman I managed to win all the swimming prizes and became captain of the cricket team. But my prowess was entirely fraudulent, or so I felt.

One event which stands out from my schooldays was my first meeting with royalty. The Prince of Wales took a personal interest in the school and paid us annual visits. One of these marked for me the beginning of what you might call a one-sided love affair with the royal family. I thought he was even more handsome than photos had led me to believe. The proceedings started with the Prince's speech. We each felt he was addressing us personally. He rounded off his talk with the observation that he envied us our education. 'In my case my educational experiences were somewhat limited,' he told us; 'that's why I was something of a slow developer in understanding the ways of the world. My family background is not always a charmed one, not when it comes to understanding other people's problems.'

He finished his talk to rousing cheers and was escorted to the dining-hall. Although it was not my day for serving at table, I nipped smartly down to the kitchen and pleaded with the chef 'Bags I serve the soup to his royal highness!' The chef answered me by handing me a silver tray loaded with brimming soup-plates. Feeling as proud as a peacock, although my hands were shaking with nerves, I bore the tray into the great dining-hall and made my way to where the Prince was seated at the top table. I was within feet of the Prince when, through a combination of awe and an over-polished floor, I slipped and fell flat on my behind. Soup-stained from head to toe, I scrambled shamefully to my feet. I caught a glimpse of the headmaster's face. If looks could kill I would have fallen dead on the spot. I looked at the Prince. He was smiling, and then, addressing my woebegone figure directly, he said in a tone loud enough for all to hear 'Don't worry, dear boy. When I am at home I always skip the soup anyway.' No wonder he was always known as 'Prince Charming'!

I did show some talent, however, while I was at Christ's, thanks to a sympathetic art master who fostered what seemed to be my one natural gift, the ability to portray anything that moved. Stubbs became my god and I used to drink him in during my many visits to the Tate. I also developed a flair for portrait painting, which is all that remains of my skill and still gives me pleasure today. But, while I loved painting horses or faces, other aspects of my art training bored me silly. For instance, if I was dispatched to do a sketch of Paddington Station or depict a glowing sunset over the Albert Hall, as likely as not I would return with an empty canvas. 'What have you been doing all afternoon?' my indignant teacher would inquire. 'I'm afraid, sir, that I fell asleep' would be my sheepish reply.

In fact, I felt no ambition to become a professional artist. Nor did it enter my head to emulate my mother and go on the stage. To be blunt, when I left Christ's Hospital at the age of eighteen I had no ambitions at all, so my father arranged for me to go along for an interview with an old friend who was a banker. Well, my business career was short – perhaps five minutes. 'How are you at maths?' asked the bank manager. 'Very poor, I'm afraid sir,' I replied. 'Good day to you!' he barked, and that was that.

More out of desperation than inspiration my father suggested I should enrol as an art student at the London Polytechnic. 'Try and make a go of it, Mike old son,' my father pleaded. 'I can only afford the fees for a year, so don't waste your time. You seem to have a talent; you must learn to apply yourself.'

But I soon found distractions to keep me away from my studies. A fellow student and I had read in the papers the sad case of an old woman whose dog was to be destroyed because she could not afford a licence. We hit on the idea of raising money by setting up our easels on the Embankment and offering to paint portraits at threepence a time. After making our pitch between two old-timers who told us to scram, we did no business at all until my pal suddenly had a bright idea. He chalked on the pavement in large letters, MONEY BACK IF NOT SATISFIED. Soon we were working away as hard as we could. An *Evening News* reporter interviewed us and took a photo which, when it appeared that night on the front page of the paper, enraged both my father and the Poly's principal. As for us, we posted a seven-and-sixpenny postal order off to the old woman and spent the rest of the money on a glorious pub crawl.

After that I found another and more exciting excuse for neglecting my studies – the opposite sex. In fact, I had fallen in love. She was a fellow student with such a stunning figure that I wished I was studying nudes, for she would have made a perfect model. My class was studying the structure of the human hand at the time, but I found it much more engrossing to hold hers in the darkness of the local cinema. Well, we played truant once too often and the principal wrote to my father asking him to remove me from his establishment as I disrupted discipline. But he was charitable enough to suggest an alternative. He said that my undoubted talent would benefit from a year's study on the Continent, adding that the language barrier might inhibit me from chatting up girls. Perhaps that was why my father chose the Belgian town of Bruges. My chief memory of Bruges is of a city full of beautiful girls who seemed to have no difficulty understanding me in any language.

But all too soon the £25 which my father had given me when I left England ran out and I realised that I had to eat. I was sitting alone in a café one night, making my cup of coffee spin out until dawn. To pass the time I started to make sketches of the other customers on the table-cloth. Then, recalling my Embankment experience, I wrote out a notice and propped it up on the table – PORTRAITS PAINTED. FIVE FRANCS. Soon there was a crowd round my table, no doubt wondering what the crazy Englishman was up to. I did a brisk trade and soon was invited to other cafés as a sort of guest artist. So at least I was sure of one meal a day, and my more motherly girl-friends were always inviting me home for others.

At the end of a year, I decided I had learned all I wanted from Belgian art, not to mention Belgian girls, and so I turned up again on the family doorstep. Father regretted that he was no longer in a position to help me. So after days of pavement pounding I landed myself a job with a commercial art firm, Garlands, where I worked in the basement in the filing department, for which I was paid ten bob a week. But once a rebel always a rebel and at lunch time I used to sneak upstairs to where the artists worked. To my delight their window overlooked Fenwick's shop window. We used to eat our sandwiches watching the shop girls undress the models. I made a very bad filing clerk and was not surprised when the kindly head of department tipped me the wink. 'Why not stall 'em and resign?' was his advice. So the next day I walked into the manager's office and announced, 'I want to hand in my notice.' 'Good,' said the paunchy manager, 'saves me the trouble of having to fire you.'

Looking back, two major forces have influenced my life. The first has been Chance, and in my mind I always give Chance the feminine gender, because the second influence has undoubtedly been the opposite sex. Not long after joining the unemployed, I was having a fish-and-chip dinner with my latest girl-friend. I had turned down an offer to dine at the Savoy at her expense, since the role of gigolo didn't appeal to me. I was wondering if I could run to a second order of chips when she said quite casually that her father had just bought shares in the new British and Dominion film studios at Elstree. 'What would you say if I got Daddy to give you an introduction to the head of the studio art department?'

Two days later I found myself en route for Elstree in Daddy's car with chauffeur and a picnic basket containing smoked salmon sandwiches and a bottle of champagne. So I can hardly say I entered the British film world through the back door. But one thing is certain. If anyone had suggested as I drove through those studio gates that one day I would become an actor, I would have told him he was out of his mind.

3
Actor by Accident

MY entry into the film world coincided with the big British film boom of the 1930s and the rise to stardom of Jessie Matthews, Tom Walls, Ralph Lynn, Gracie Fields, Jack Buchanan and Leslie Howard. The leading British producer at the time was Herbert Wilcox, who had just built Britain's most up-to-date studios at Elstree, and the papers were full of news about his latest discovery, a young chorus girl called Anna Neagle.

Despite the grand manner of my arrival, I was quickly brought down to earth by the studio art director. He explained that there was a temporary lull in production. At least, that was the excuse he made for telling me that there were no vacancies for a would-be designer. Probably to get rid of me, he came up with an alternative suggestion: 'Why don't you apply for a job as an extra? That way you could earn a pound a day.'

Now, to one used to getting by on ten bob a week a pound a day seemed a fortune and the job would also give me the invaluable opportunity of studying the construction of film sets at first hand. 'How do I sign on?' I asked. With great relief, the art chief directed me to the casting office.

'I'm looking for crowd work,' I said, thinking it best to come straight to the point. The casting manager, a harassed little man peering through horn-rimmed glasses, said unexpectedly 'How tall are you?' 'Six foot one.' 'Ah!'

he beamed, 'just the right height.' 'Just the right height for what?' I inquired. 'How would you like a job as Douglas Fairbanks junior's stand-in?' he replied.

I discovered soon enough that there is nothing more boring than standing for hours while the camera is set up for the star to come and step into your shoes. I will never forget my first day on a film set. The film was *Catherine the Great* and starred, besides Doug junior, the great German actress Elisabeth Bergner and a luscious young redhead, Diana Napier. So I found myself sitting with this dish in a scanty negligée perched on my knee. We had to rehearse a passionate clinch, during which the lady responded with real-life ardour. I would have enjoyed every minute of it except that all through the shooting shadowing Diana's every move was a tubby teddy bear of a man who spoke English with a thick German accent. He was Richard Tauber and he and Diana had just announced their engagement.

However, my most lasting impression of that day was one of bewilderment. Every time I walked on the set the great Bergner screamed some unintelligible word in my direction. When I got home my father asked me how I had got on. 'I'm not sure,' I replied, and repeated Bergner's mysterious screams. My father laughed 'What a fool you are, Mike. That's your name in Russian. That's what they used to call you in Moscow!'

My beginner's luck, alas, deserted me. For my next job, I found myself merely an extra. Every morning I used to catch the milk train to Elstree, then plod through the rain to the studios in company with my fellow slaves. I remember the vow I made at that time: 'If ever I am rich enough to own a car, I will give poor sods like myself a lift!' Years later I did become rich enough to own a car – a coach-built Rolls. At the end of each day there used to be a queue waiting for me at the studio gates, anyone from the humblest extra to the make-up man or the assistant director. They would all pile into what became known as the 'Wilding bus' and we would make the journey back to

My mother as a young actress
th Sir Ben Greet's theatre
mpany

4   Me at eight in my much-hated
school uniform

5   Art student in Bruges

6   With Fay Compton in *Tonight at 8.30*

7   With Kay, shortly after our marriage

8 A rustic role, in
The Farmer's Wife

9 A spot of mayhem
from one of my naval
comedies, *Sailors Three*

10 Ratings resigned – Tommy Trinder, Claude Hulbert and myself in *Sailors Three*

11 I was cast in the role John Gielgud played on the stage in *Dear Octopus* – but, alas, David Hemmings stole this scene

12   *Dear Octopus* – addressing the family, my marathon speech

13   *Piccadilly Incident* – the first love scene I played with Anna

14 *Piccadilly Incident* – with Anna and A. E. Matthews

5 In *Carnival,* with Sally Gray. The film got the bird but I didn't, although I was head over heels in love with her.

16 *The Courtneys of Curzon Street* – my second picture with Anna and Herbert, in which I played a lord who falls in love with an Irish parlourmaid

17 *The Courtneys of Curzon Street* – love triumphs over class. In the end Anna and I are married.

18 Anna and I learning our lines on the set of *Spring in Park Lane*.

London in comfort, stopping for several 'quickies' at pubs en route.

My career has been filled with coincidences, but none has been stranger or luckier than my first role as an extra in *Bitter Sweet*, directed by Herbert Wilcox and starring Anna Neagle. Herbert commanded the loyalty of all of us – unlike some directors, who treated extras like sheep. Herbert used to address us as 'Ladies and Gentlemen' and would always take the trouble to explain our role in the scene. As a result, every man jack of us gave of our best.

I have never ceased to look upon it as a miracle that we three should have met this way. What is more, there was an immediate affinity between us. It so happened that I was one of twenty young men called on to take part in what was supposed to be a roaring-twenties party. The assistant director had paired off all the other young men to dance with pretty girls but, when it came to my turn, he said 'You dance with him', and pointed to a willowy young man. I protested 'Why should I dance with a man with all these pretty young girls around? What kind of a man do you think I am?' At this moment, Herbert came up and wanted to know what all the fuss was about. When I explained, he fell about laughing. 'Of course you shall have a pretty girl, Mr Wilding,' he said. He patted me on the back and said 'Just to put you in the mood, come along to Miss Neagle's dressing-room and we'll give you a glass of champagne.'

Mercifully, my days as an extra were short, but I soon learned to respect and admire my fellow slaves for their stamina and good humour, which never left them although they might be on call from eight in the morning until midnight.

People often ask me about my feelings during that early part of my career. How and when did I decide to take acting seriously? The answer is that I never made any such decision. It was made for me as usual by a lady – a complete stranger whose name I do not know to this day.

One night I was watching a rather boring play at the Westminster Theatre. I rushed to the bar during the interval and was lingering over my second drink when a lady came up to me and said 'Are you an actor? If not, you ought to be. You have the looks.' I replied that to date I had only succeeded in reaching the dubious status of a film extra. 'That's no way to become an actor,' was her brisk reply; 'you ought to join a repertory company.' I thought she was either a little mad or pulling my leg, so asked with tongue in cheek 'Do you have any particular company in mind?' 'Yes,' she replied promptly, 'the Watford Rep are always looking for juveniles.'

The very next morning I took a train to Watford. There were twenty other contestants lined up on the stage. We were asked to read a three-minute piece from *Accent on Youth*. One by one, the other hopefuls were dismissed with that all too familiar phrase – 'We'll let you know.' I was the last to go on stage and was so nervous I rattled through the piece, and was walking off the stage when I heard a shout from the stalls: 'Hey, you. Come back!' The voice came from the stage director, who told me to come out front and join him. 'You'll do,' he said off-handedly. 'Full of nerves. But that's not always a bad thing.' Then he offered me a year's contract.

I could not believe my luck and arrived next morning for rehearsals feeling rather like a fraud who would soon be found out. And so I was. The stage director's voice bellowed at me 'Speak up, young man! I can't hear a word you're saying and I'm sitting in the stalls. How do you think you'll be heard in the gallery? Haven't you any idea of voice projection?'

'I'm afraid not sir,' I faltered, 'I'm sorry.'

'Well,' threatened the stage director, 'you'd better learn something about it by the end of the week or I'll have to fire you!'

I remained at Watford for a year, gradually learning my trade and taking on bigger parts. I became aware, for the first time, what a difficult art acting was. On my last night at the rep a gentleman who looked like a navvy but spoke with an Oxbridge accent came backstage and introduced himself as an agent. He predicted that a promising career awaited me if I became his client. 'Just say the word,' he promised, 'and I'll get you an audition for C. B. Cochran's next production.' Next day I went along for the audition and landed a small part in Cochran's latest revue, *Home and Beauty*. Thus begun my career as a West End actor.

If I make it sound easy, I can only say that's the way it was. I just took life one day, one part, at a time and never seemed to be out of work. For this piece of luck I owe a tremendous debt to C. B. Cochran who gave me parts in all his early revues. Alas, my roles were too small to bring me into direct contact with the great man himself. But Cocky's wit and showmanship were already legendary. My favourite story concerns the redecoration of the Palace Theatre. The designer asked him 'How would you like the seats covered, Mr Cochran?' 'With backsides,' Cocky replied.

By far the most memorable personality I worked with was the beautiful Dorothy Dickson. Quite by chance I became her leading man, because Richard Dolman refused to go on unless he got co-star billing. Now Dorothy, for all her feminine fragility, was too tough a character to give in to such blackmail. So I was picked from twenty other contenders to partner her in singing and dancing the famous number, 'These Foolish Things'. I protested that I couldn't sing and had never danced a step on the stage, but Dot was adamant. 'I know you can do it,' she bullied me, 'you have style.'

During rehearsals I developed such a crush on her that I asked the stage director if I could kiss her at the end of the number. 'Why do you want to kiss her?' he demanded. I replied 'Because she is so beautiful, of course!' Well, I got my way, and on the first night at the end of the number, I kissed her through the 'scrim'. Throughout the duet we were separated by a kind of gauze known as a scrim, which gave a kind of hazy look to the scene, but which in reality is made of harsh wire. As I kissed her, the wire cut into my nose. I had a red nose every night for the six months of the run, but I didn't care. I thought 'How lucky can you get?' — *and* I got my first favourable press notices as a result of that number. But how could anyone go wrong with such a song and such a magical co-star?

Before my name became at all well known, I was 'discovered' and hastily discarded three times. The first discovery had directed me into rep. About the second discovery I am a little hazy. All I remember is that one night while I was playing a small part in a straight play starring Eric Portman, a young man appeared at my dressing-room door. 'My name is Anthony Pelissier,' he announced, 'and I am looking for a juvenile lead to accompany my mother on her forthcoming tour of Australia.' 'Who is your mother?' I asked. I felt about two inches high when he replied 'Fay Compton'. Two weeks later she paid me a visit and came straight to the point. 'I am offering you a year's contract to tour Australia with my company, playing the juvenile lead. Would you be interested?' Interested! I was in a daze of delight. She invited me to dine with her at the Savoy, but I was so overawed that I hardly uttered a word throughout the meal.

I shall never forget that year-long Australian tour, nor the great actress who made it possible. And I remember to this day one notice from a leading Melbourne theatre critic about my small part in the opening play of our tour, *Victoria Regina*: 'The most finished performance of the evening was given by Michael Wilding in the relatively small role of Prince Ernst. His presence lights up the whole stage.' It was this notice that gave me my first real motivation to become as good an actor as I could.

I shall always be indebted to Fay for her patience, guidance and above all encouragement during that Australian adventure, and for a marvellous hint she gave me about timing. She was sitting on the beach watching me while I was surf-boarding. I got to be quite expert at it, but sometimes I would hit a wave head-on instead of riding it. Afterwards Fay said to me 'You know how you time the crest of each wave? Well, that's how you must time audience response. It's all a matter of a split second. Come in too soon with a line and you'll drown. Come in too late and you'll fall flat on your face. Every laugh, every reaction from the audience must be caught at its crest. Just like a wave.'

On my return to England, I found that the magic name of Compton opened many doors and got me the offer of a part in a film which I would gladly forget, except that it brought about a memorable encounter with a famous name from the silent screen, Mabel Poulton. The film, misnamed *Symphony Pastoral*, was a frenzied exercise in incompetence by all concerned and was never publicly shown. And no wonder! The director insisted on the action being fortified by a full orchestra playing Beethoven's Pastoral Symphony, and the wretched cast were asked to act to a metronome. I would have forgotten the whole episode had I not learned of the personal tragedy of Mabel Poulton. She had been as big a star as Mary Pickford, but with the coming of sound had been defeated by her pronounced Cockney accent. She told me she had engaged an elocution teacher to improve her diction. But, alas, his lessons were to no avail and she retired from the screen, which was a great loss to the public, as anyone old enough to remember her elfin charm would agree.

My return from Australia coincided with Chamberlain's return from Munich and the newspapers were full of talk about 'peace for our time'. The national mood of relief mixed with wishful thinking was reflected in the sudden popularity of revue, based on witty songs and sketches with a topical flavour, which brought to the public such talents as Ian Carmichael, Walter Crisham, and the one and only Hermione Gingold. I was lucky enough to be invited to join the company at the Gate Theatre, which everyone regarded as the *crème de la crème* of revue.

The mood of the players backstage matched that of our audiences – laugh, clown, laugh, and the devil take tomorrow. So every night during that last summer of peace, we went on stage, singing topical songs and cracking gags about Hitler, Mussolini and Chamberlain in an effort to fool ourselves and our audience into ignoring the obviously unavoidable catastrophe of the Second World War.

4
Love and Bombs

IN 1938 I found myself falling in love again, but this time it was more than the usual passing fancy. The object of my affection was also my co-star at the Gate, a highly talented artist called Kay Young, who possessed a strong dramatic beauty not unlike that of a young Joan Crawford. Our first meeting was not exactly romantic. We collided as we were coming out of the same agent's office. Kay said that for her it was a matter of love at first sight, but I was my usual dithering self and it was not like that for me.

However, I must have been struck by her looks, for there and then I asked her to join me for a drink and she accepted. I was so surprised that I led her into the first door we came to, the entrance to a cheap Leicester Square café, and we ordered the wine of the day – tomato juice. It was not exactly a romantic beginning, nor I fear did I turn out to be a model suitor during the weeks that followed. I never sent her flowers, bought her perfume or showered her with compliments, except to admit grudgingly that she was one of the few women who could make me laugh.

In short, I was terrified of my own emotions. At last I had met a girl I could not easily forget. Indeed, after knowing her for a while I could not think of life without her. But not a word did I utter to this effect. It was Kay who made the running, and if I remember correctly it was Kay who finally proposed. Like all women who have figured in my life, before or since, Kay was the dominant partner. It was Kay who used to boost my professional morale with remarks like 'One day you are going to be a big star. I feel it in my bones.' 'Suppose I turn out to be a flop?' I countered. 'You wouldn't want to be married to a failure, would you?' 'No,' she replied promptly, 'but I know a good thing when I see it. That's why I'm nabbing you now before you get too popular!'

And so we were married. Besides my father and mother, who were delighted that I was at last settling down, only Kay's relations were present. Kay found us a not too expensive top-floor studio flat in South Kensington. It amused us very much at the time that the *Tatler* devoted a full page spread to us and described us as an 'exclusive Kensington couple'.

The only exclusive feature of our new habitat was the fact that the flat opposite was occupied by Noel Coward. Often at night, after the theatre; we would take our beer and sandwiches up to the flat roof and, because Coward always used to leave the top-storey windows open, we were able to eavesdrop on various impromptu cabaret acts performed by visiting celebrities, our favourite being Marlene Dietrich.

I have only happy memories of that long, last hot summer of peace. But Kay, as always, was much more of a realist than I was. She knew our roof-top flat would not be a very safe haven once the bombs started falling. Nevertheless, that is exactly where we found ourselves that September morning when the sirens first sounded.

Like all other London theatres, the Gate temporarily closed with the blackout and at my urging Kay went to stay with relatives in the country. I missed her terribly and with all speed set about finding us a safer place to live. By luck, my landlord came up with an offer of a basement flat in the same building. This sounded much safer and I took it at once, telephoning Kay the good news. We had been separated for three months and in retrospect that did not get our marriage off to a good start. I fear that during her absence I strayed from the straight and narrow. Just the same, I was overjoyed to have her back.

On the night of her return, I arrived home to find Kay sitting on a rug in front of the fireplace. At that second, I heard a stick of bombs falling. To say I heard it is incorrect. There was just a whooshing sound. Then a crash. A barrel of soot poured down the chimney. Kay, who had been kneeling, her head between her knees, lifted her face and I laughed. 'You look just like a Black and White Minstrel,' I said. She laughed back 'I've always wanted to play in *Uncle Tom's Cabin.*'

There were no lights. All our windows were shattered. I noticed that Kay's hands were trembling violently. 'Come on,' I urged, 'let's go round to the pub. We could both use a drink.' Kay clung to my arm, still trembling as we groped our way along the blacked-out street. Suddenly, we collided with what seemed like a mother's meeting, to judge from feminine laughter in the darkness.

'Make way for his royal highness!' shouted a voice and in the sudden flash of the ARP warden's torch I saw the famous face of one lately in the news as a VIP war refugee. It was the Emperor Haile Selassie and behind him, arrayed in exotic robes, were his seven wives.

I bowed low. 'Your Royal Highness,' I said, 'I beg you and yours to do us the honour of joining us for a drink.' A serene smile lit up the handsome face. 'I thank you,' he replied in perfect English, 'and my wives thank you. But not even Hitler's bombs will tempt us to imbibe alcohol.' And so saying, he and his beautiful spouses followed the ARP warden into the safety of an air-raid shelter.

At last we reached our local. I asked the landlord 'Where did the bombs fall?' He replied 'On you, I think.' 'I think not,' I replied. 'Here we are. Safe and sound.' We had not one but several drinks, and then, feeling much warmer in our tummies, groped our way home.

We had to climb over a pile of fallen masonry to reach our front door. By that time the police, the fire brigade and the ARP had arrived. The warden asked for permission to enter the premises. 'Welcome to Liberty hall,' I said, and it was an apt welcome, for the hallway ceiling was a gaping hole into the sky above us. Kay began to lead the way down stairs, but when we reached the halfway landing I suddenly felt the urgent call of nature. Above us the whole house had been blown away be a direct hit, but the door marked WC was unscathed. I excused myself and went in. Having been brought up properly, I naturally concluded things by pulling the chain. It didn't work. I pulled and tugged and still no joy. So finally I gave up and left it.

When I went up to the WC the next morning, I nearly passed out. I opened the door to see that the lavatory was hanging on by one frail pipe over a deep chasm down to the basement.

Like everyone else, Kay and I tried to treat the blitz as a bad joke until it brought tragedy. Kay had always been very close to her mother and I soon shared her affection and admiration for this entirely lovable woman. She was as brave as a lion and as stubborn as a mule and, despite all Kay's entreaties, she refused to move from her basement flat in the City. No bloody Germans were going to drive her out of the home where she had lived all her life. One night a bomb went clean through the lift shaft, destroying the building from top floor to basement, and Kay's mother was reported missing. Kay was in a terrible state, so I volunteered to go along and identify the body.

The mortuary was not far from St Paul's. It was a bizarre sight. There were acres of desolation, with nothing else standing except this house of death, clean, pristine, and untouched. A great brass plate on the door glittered in the sunlight proclaiming what it was. I rang the bell and a man opened the door. He was rather bent with age and his clothing and hands were flecked with fluid.

'I've come to identify a body,' I said. 'Have you now?' he replied. 'Where from?' I told him my mother-in-law's address. He said 'Well, there are no bodies at all from that building. Only bits. Do you want to see some bits?' I said 'In that case, I suppose so.' He disappeared and came back a few minutes later carrying a sack over his shoulder, and sticking out of the top I recognised a boot. A very small woman's boot, which I remembered Kay's mother wearing. I said 'I can identify the owner of that little black boot. She was my mother-in-law.' He put down the sack and said 'Sorry, Guv. But she wouldn't have suffered any.' Then he carefully wiped his hands on the edge of the sack and gave me a final handshake.

After her mother's death something of the joy of life seemed to die in Kay, as, alas, it did in our marriage. But war or no war, separations or no separations, I think it would have petered out sooner or later. We had no fights or recriminations. And, although our parting was amicable enough, I was miserably aware that the breakdown of our marriage after three years had been entirely my fault. I was nobody's idea of an ideal mate and, although I was too ashamed to do so at the time, in retrospect I take all the blame for the failure of a marriage to a very wonderful person who deserved a better husband.

5

Not Looking at the Camera

I WANTED to follow in my father's footsteps and join the Army. So three days after war broke out I went to the nearest recruiting station where, when presented with the 'capabilities' form, I wanted to put down 'camouflage', but found that I could not spell it. As it turned out, this was of little consequence, as I failed the medical and was turned down as 'unfit for military service'. This rejection rankled deeply. I felt useless and unwanted. At that time it seemed as though London theatres would remain closed indefinitely, so there was not even the consolation of work. Then my agent asked me to come round to his office and told me that since so many players were being called up there might be an opening for me in films.

Agents sometimes spot the obvious before their fellow men. Not often, but sometimes. In fact, I felt like the character in Evelyn Waugh's novel *Put Out More Flags* of whom another bloke says 'Wasn't he lucky to have a war to do well in?' Had not the cream of my profession plus any up-and-coming rivals been called up, my entry into the film world would never have been so easy nor my climb to success so swift. But, when my agent landed me my first job in an Ealing comedy starring Tommy Trinder, I still had mixed feelings about acting for the screen. Even as an extra I had been torn by two sensations: the technique fascinated me, but the idea of doing it terrified me. Paradoxically enough, assistant directors were always shouting at me 'Don't look at the camera!' They must be mad, I thought, I'm much too terrified to look at the camera. I cut it dead, pretended it wasn't there.

My first film break, with Tommy Trinder, was a stroke of luck. Some comedians reserve all their humour for the public. There are precious few, like Trinder, who cannot help being funny all the time. With that wonderful long-jawed slab of Cockney humour around, it was easier to push my nerves into the background.

On our first day's shooting I had lunch with him in the studio canteen. There was a telephone by the cash desk and it seemed to have an odd fascination for him. Every time it rang he leapt to his feet, picked up the receiver and said at the top of his voice 'Ealing Eating 'Ouse 'ere!' and tried to persuade the unfortunate person on the other end of the line that he was silly to want to talk to Sir Michael Balcon when Tommy Trinder was at his service.

My next break was being cast in *Tilly of Bloomsbury*, where I met another great comedian, the portly, Yorkshire-accented Sydney Howard. Now nobody would have cast Sydney in the role of a ladies' man since he had a large, sad, full moon of a face, a balding pate and a figure like a toby jug. Sydney's words of greeting to me were 'I hear you're quite a chap with the ladies?' 'From what I hear,' I replied, 'you don't do badly yourself!' Syd winked. 'When we have a moment I'll tell you my secret.'

Sure enough, during the first shooting break in the day he took my arm and led me to his dressing-room. 'Remember,' he cautioned, 'this is to be our little secret,' and so saying he opened the drawer of his dressing-table and brought forth a small brown bottle. 'Just look at the label,' he said proudly. It read 'Meg's Magic Medicine' and in small letters underneath was the direction: 'To be taken in cases of impotence to increase virility'.

Then he told me how about ten years previously a chum, thinking Sydney was not getting the best out of life, took him to a Mayfair brothel. Sydney paid his fiver and was shown upstairs to where a half-naked female lay invitingly on a large double bed. 'I was out of my clothes before you could say lightning,' Syd recalled, 'and climbed in beside her. Then, what do you think happened? Bloody wars! I couldn't even raise my big toe!'

The lady advised him to go and see Meg, a herbalist well known for her treatment of sexual disabilities. She gave him the medicine, which he took for a week before going back to see the lady. 'Bloody wars! Even though it's me that says it, I did her proud! I've been taking the stuff ever since and never looked back.'

Then to my horror he poured out half a tumbler and handed it to me. At first I declined, saying that so far I had felt no such need, but he retorted 'The day may come, Mike laddie, when you'll thank me for this.' I felt it would be ungracious to disagree and took a sip and nearly choked to death. 'What the hell is in this bloody mixture?' 'That's Meg's secret,' replied Sydney. 'Do what I do. Swallow it in one.'

Back on the set, my stomach started making strange noises, so loud that they were picked up by the microphone. I began to feel more queasy with every take and at the earliest opportunity rushed off the set and drove home at speed. On arriving the first thing I did was to ring up a particularly heavy date I had that night and cry off because of acute indigestion. Then I was heartily sick. Needless to say, I never resorted to Meg's medicine again.

Tilly of Bloomsbury brought my name for the first time to the attention of the critics, notably in the magazine *Picturegoer*. 'If pressed,' the reviewer wrote, 'we would say that Michael Wilding is the best thing in the picture. He plays Perce, an exuberant, always charming, Cockney: a role so often misunderstood and patronisingly played by West End actors. But Mr Wilding never guys the role.'

In fact, playing Cockneys was as easy as breathing, because I used to laugh and work and drink with them. I found they had a sense of humour like nobody else's. Above all, I respected them for their independence and generosity of spirit.

In my early Ealing days, I found two types brought me luck – Cockneys and sailors, and sometimes a combination of both. I played a Cockney in naval gear in three films in a row, starting with *Convoy*. Then came a comedy, *Sailors Don't Care,* starring Claude Hulbert, whom I have always admired for overcoming the handicap of having as his brother the more famous Jack, who had established a niche for himself as the perfect silly fool. I cared deeply about this film, as I did about all the films I made at Ealing. Although still haunted by camera nerves, I was now thoroughly bitten by the film bug and worked hard to make a success of things. But had it not been for the faith of one director, Charles Frend, my career at Ealing might have come to an abrupt end. I was beginning to feel in danger of being type-cast, so was delighted when my agent called to say he thought he could land me the part of Glynis Johns's lover in the thriller *Cottage to Let.*

Next day I went down to the studios and did a test with the enchanting, husky-voiced Glynis. After the test I was relaxing with Glynis in the canteen, trying to summon up the nerve to ask her for a date, when over the tannoy I was called to Charles Frend's office. As soon as I came through the door I could sense there was something wrong. 'Balcon has just seen your test,' he said grimly. 'And?' I inquired nerviously. 'And,' continued Frend, 'he asked me your name. When I told him, he stood up and said "Tell Mr Wilding to go away and not to come back until he has learned his job!" '

Frend smiled. 'Don't look so woebegone,' he said, patting me on the shoulder. 'I'm casting you just the same. Mick can go and jump in the lake. I know quality when I see it. That's what I'm paid for. If I am wrong, then he can fire me. But I'm giving you the chance. So don't let me down.'

In fact, the film gave me fresh faith in myself. The day after it opened I was in the studio canteen when I was told to report immediately to Sir Michael's office. Feeling butterflies at the bottom of my stomach, I knocked at his door. 'Come in,' said a chilly voice. I walked in. 'Sit down,' commanded Balcon, and he fixed me with a long hard stare. Just when I was ready to sweat, he said casually 'Haven't I seen your face somewhere before?' 'Yes,' I replied, taking the plunge. 'After seeing my film test you told me to go away and not come back until I had learned my job.' Balcon didn't blink an eyelid. 'Well,' he said in that dry emotionless voice of his, 'judging by what I saw last night you have gone some way in that direction. But you still have got a long way to go in diplomacy. Never tell a producer he cannot recognise talent. Not everyone would be prepared to eat their words!'

My next assignment at Ealing was again in a naval role, but this time I moved to the upper deck in a film in which John Clements was the star. *Ships with Wings* was based on the story of the *Ark Royal*. This was my first meeting with Clements, who turned out to be the most generous of actors and has since become one of my closest friends. I discovered his wonderful sense of humour on the first day of shooting; 'Of course, in this film, I die in the end. In every film I've ever made, I die before the final fade-out. Maybe that's why the critics are so kind to me. I'm already embalmed in their imagination.'

Ships starred Ann Todd and Jane Baxter. By coincidence I had been fag to Jane's brother at school and had adored her then. I thought her dazzlingly pretty and it seemed only poetic justice that in the film I 'got the girl in the end'. *Ships* was Ealing's most ambitious war film to date. It was supposed to do for the Navy what *Target For Tonight* had done for the Air Force and, quite by accident, it brought me my biggest break to date.

Shortly after the première I dropped in one lunch time to The Ivy. Halfway through the meal, Noel Coward strode over to my table, and shook me warmly by the hand. 'You were absolutely marvellous in that film,' he said. 'Which film, sir?' I asked. 'Ships with something,' he replied. 'You were so obviously an officer and a gentleman. Will you please come and work with me on my new film, *In Which We Serve?*' 'Why sir,' I replied, 'it would be an honour.'

This meeting was the beginning of a long and warm friendship which lasted until the end of the Master's life. I was privileged to hear many of his witticisms at first hand and cannot resist repeating a Cowardism related to me by Hermione Gingold. She had been in the recording studio when Noel cut the disc of 'Don't Put Your Daughter on the Stage, Mrs Worthington'. Coward fluffed the first take and turning to his male producer said in ringing tones 'I certainly fucked that up!' Then, with a swift bow to his entirely female studio audience, he said 'Ladies, pray pardon the "up"!'

But Coward was deadly serious when preparing his Navy film. 'There must be nothing inconsistent or vulgar about the film,' he told the press, 'or I should be forever ashamed. I am trying to make a dignified tribute to the Royal Navy.' Before even a word of the script was written, Coward had obtained full co-operation from the Admiralty to bring to the screen the true story of the destroyer *Kelly*, from its launching to its sinking off Crete, and to add to the realism Coward had enlisted as actors the soldiers and sailors who had actually served with the destroyer's heroic crew.

When shooting began at Korda's studios in Denham, everyone involved in the production agreed that the star of the film was the life-size model of the *Kelly*. It was the biggest set ever built in any British studio, and thanks to ingenious electrical devices it could list sixteen degrees in either direction.

On the first day of shooting I barely recognised the Master, wearing a tattered naval uniform, covered in oil from head to foot. The cast, which included John Mills and Bernard Miles, was in a continual state of discomfort. We were supposed to be bombed and machine-gunned as we clung to a raft in the studio tank. Crude oil was spread on top of the water, then some misguided soul decided we should not freeze and turned on the water heater full blast. The stand-ins went in first and let out an almighty yelp. The oil on top of the water prevented the steam from escaping and the water itself seemed nearly at boiling-point. However, the film was costing more than £1,000 a day, so there was no time to be wasted waiting for the water to cool. Noel and the rest of us lowered our bodies into the tank inch by inch, and boiled! Afterwards we figured we had all lost a stone in weight during the week it took to film those scenes.

That was one occasion when I did not shake hands with the king and queen! Noel had invited King George VI and Queen Elizabeth down to the studios for the day. After showing them some rushes, Coward ushered the royal couple on to the set, while we players, still covered in stinking black oil, stood at attention, waiting to be introduced. Noel saved the day; after taking one look at us, he said, bowing deeply, 'I hope that Your Majesties will excuse the cast from shaking hands?' King George grinned. 'Judging by the smell,' he replied, 'they will be doing us a favour!'

This was the first film Noel directed and he guarded his privacy like a monk. No visitors were allowed on the set and this included the press. I did not know enough about film directors at that time to judge his mastery, but one thing was certain – he was a martinet about actors learning their lines. One leading player was sacked on the first day because he was not word-perfect. In those days, heaven be praised, I had a photographic memory, but this did not stop Coward putting me through my paces a dozen times before he was satisfied with the results. No wonder it took six months to film and that towards the end I was becoming so bored I was only too glad when it was all over. Very few actors would confess to being bored while being directed by Coward, but unfortunately I have always had a low boredom threshold – and what other actor would have run away from a chance to appear in Terence Rattigan's latest masterpiece?

In 1944 I had only met Rattigan casually, so I was startled and flattered when one day the phone rang and it was Terry. 'I have just finished a new play. It's called *While the Sun Shines*. There is a young character in it about twenty-one. He's an earl. I think you would suit it down to the ground.' 'It's a long time since I was twenty-one,' I protested. 'I know,' he replied, 'but I can't find anyone of that age suitable to play the part.'

So I agreed to meet him half an hour later at the Ritz bar. Terry's first words to me were 'This is the longest part I have ever written.' I had not been on the stage for five years in a legit part; so, without bothering to wait and finish my dry martini, I bolted. But I had forgotton that Terry was a double blue. He chased me all the way to the nearest bus-stop, caught up with me, and dragged me back to the Ritz. After half an hour of Terry's charm I gave in and said I would give it a try.

The play ran for four years, but as usual boredom caught up with me and I bowed out after six months, despite the fact that I had the chance of playing with Ronald Squire. Squire was unique. His timing and charm, his flair for turning the most innocent line into a saucy nuance were nothing short of perfection. I was much too shy, of course, to let on to him about my hero-worship. You can imagine my delight on the last night when Terry came round to my dressing-room. 'I'll be sorry to see you go, old chum,' he said, 'but not half as sorry as Ronnie Squire. You know what he just said to me about you?' 'No,' I said, with a sinking feeling inside, 'what am I doing wrong?' Terry laughed. 'In Ronnie's eyes you can do no wrong. He said "I hope, if I have a comedy mantel worth bestowing on anyone, it may fall on young Wilding's shoulders."' News of a knighthood could not have given me more pleasure.

I also left the play because I was suddenly in steady demand to act in films. My agent, knowing my fear of financial insecurity, was quick to point out that films spelled bigger money in a shorter time. I returned to Ealing Studios and found myself cast in Terry Rattigan's *English Without Tears*, which featured the French actor Claude Dauphin, who used to perfect his English by insisting on helping me do the *Times* crossword. I can never think of Claude without recalling one of the most delightful surprises of my life – something only a Frenchman could think up.

It happened five years later, when I was a star and so rich that I had bought a half share in a boat with Stewart Granger. One day when we were sailing up a canal en route for Paris, Stewart was becoming very bad-tempered about the delay in getting through the numerous locks. Worse was yet to come. At the stroke of seven in the evening all the locks were closed and we were still forty miles from Paris, Stewart said 'Bugger the lock-keepers! Let's abandon ship and hire a car!'

When we arrived in Paris about an hour later Stewart told the driver to pull up at a rather grand hotel. 'Stay where you are,' he said. 'I'll go and fix accommodation.' Five minutes later he emerged looking very cross indeed. Whether they had frowned on him in his open-necked shirt and blue jeans I do not know, but there was definitely no room at the inn. Stewart dismissed the car and suggested we stroll up the Champs-Élysées to his favourite hotel, the Georges Cinq. I had my doubts whether this august establishment would take a kinder view of his appearance. But I had learned better than to argue with Stewart once he had set his mind on something. We had just reached the entrance to the hotel when I saw a familiar figure lounging on the front steps. A second later I was being embraced in a bear-hug and kissed violently on both cheeks. It was Claude Dauphin.

'What on earth are you doing here, and why is your friend looking so cross?' he asked. I explained our predicament. Claude grinned and winked. 'I will soon put you both in a better humour,' he declared. Then, whispering in my ear, he added 'I have two girls up in my room. Follow me! Bet you and your friend will find it hard which one to choose!' If I hadn't been so glad to see him I wouldn't have followed him. I was hardly in the mood. 'Voilà!' he cried, and with a theatrical gesture flung open the door. The sight that met my eyes made me feel I must be dreaming. Seated side by side on the couch in the middle of the room were the two sex queens of the era, Hedy Lamarr and Rita Hayworth. Claude was right. It was hard to know which to choose, but for me the odds were slightly in favour of Hayworth, as I knew she was such a wonderful dancer. Stewart and Hedy might have known each other all their lives; and Claude, bless his Gallic heart, played odd man out while showing us a night on the town I shall never forget.

To return to blacked-out Britain, I was next cast in H. G. Wells's *Kipps*, thanks to the call-up of John Mills, and so worked with that brilliant film director Carol Reed. We eventually shot the film at Shepherd's Bush Studios, where Carol organised parties of roof-spotters to sound the alarm when bombers were directly overhead, thus reducing the time lost on our daily shooting schedule.

It was evident to me, as it was to all who worked with him, that Carol was headed for the heights. But the quality which struck me most forcibly was that he knew what had mass appeal. Carol always offered me a lift to and from work, and as we reached the studio gates he would lean out of the car window and call to the gate-keeper 'Hey, George, what do you think of the film so far?' He always made a point of asking employees like George to view his daily rushes. 'If you'll forgive me saying so, sir,' replied the gate-keeper, 'not too much. In fact the scene I saw today was perfectly rotten!'

The next morning as we drove through the studio gates, Carol rolled down the window and called 'George, old boy. I've been thinking about what you said last night. You've liked the film so far. What was wrong with that scene?' George scratched his head and looked shamefaced. 'It must be my ignorance, sir. But I didn't like the scene where everyone goes round with letters pasted on their backs. Couldn't make head nor tail of it.'

George was referring to a scene where the guests at a party sport anagrams of their names on their backs. It was one of my favourite scenes in the picture, but being a crossword fan I'm a sucker for anagrams. That morning Carol called the whole cast together. 'We are going to re-shoot the party scene,' he announced. 'I am rewriting it and throwing out the anagram jokes. I feel the general public will not be amused.

6
Gib and Jobbing

THE war brought many ups and downs. After I had finished filming with Carol Reed, once again Chance stepped in and offered me an opportunity, which – though brief – brought me a great deal of satisfaction However, I only learned recently how close I came to missing it. Binkie Beaumont, head of the powerful H. M. Tennant organisation, had offered to put something together for Basil Dean's ENSA group to entertain the servicemen posted on the beleaguered Rock of Gibraltar. At the last minute, owing to his service commitments, John Mills had to drop out. Binkie phoned John Clements to ask him to suggest a replacement. 'I had no hesitation in putting forward your name,' John told me. 'But Binkie would have none of you. Said you were not a big enough name. I told him, having played with you in two films, I was convinced you were a big enough talent.' At last, after considerable nagging from John, Binkie gave in and I found myself with twenty-four hours to pack my bags and prepare to fly to Gibraltar.

The company was headed by John Gielgud, along with Edith Evans, Elizabeth Welsh, Beatrice Lillie and Jeanne de Casalis. They had all had the advantage of a preliminary tour in the provinces, whereas I was thrown in at the deep end, not knowing what was expected of me and wondering if I could hold my own in such a star-spangled cast.

An RAF bomber flew us to the Rock. On arrival there was a momentary panic when we could not find our costumes and props, which were supposed to have preceded us by sea. But after searching all day, we found them under 900 tons of mixed cargo on a merchant ship. The Rock had an almost peace-like feel about it. For one thing, there was no blackout and we were able to sunbathe in the warm Mediterranean weather. We gave three shows a day, on ships, in hospital wards and in army camps, where we found the troops on top of the world as news of Montgomery's successes in North Africa had just filtered through.

After rehearsals, in which I was accidentally very funny, Jeanne de Casalis, who had become famous in a radio character sketch as 'Mrs Feather', came up to me and drawled 'My dear Mike, you are missing your vocation. You are a born stand-up comic. Why not join my act? You would knock 'em dead on the vaudeville circuits.' 'Thanks for the offer, Jeanne,' I replied, 'but I'm not a born comic – only lucky enough sometimes to get my audiences laughing with me.' 'Maybe you're right,' she said, 'but if you're ever out of a job, remember, Mrs Feather would like to hear from you.' I gave her a great big hug and said 'I shall remember that offer with pride.'

I was sharing a dressing-room with John Gielgud, who as well as being one of the world's greatest actors is in my opinion as near a saint as anyone I have ever met. His outstanding quality is his humility, which was brought home to me by an incident during our Gib tour. John was playing in a sketch about either Hitler or Mussolini. On the first night, he played it straight, and so great was the applause and laughter that I fancy John, who had never played this type of comedy before, must have got carried away. Anyway, the next night, he not only donned a funny uniform and adopted a funny walk, he was what we call in the profession reaching for laughs – and none came.

After the performance he returned to our dressing-room completely downcast. He appealed to me: 'It went down fine on the first night. What am I doing wrong? You know about comedy. I don't.' Hesitantly I put forward the theory that the audience sensed he was reaching for laughs and when they do that it is usually fatal. They dry up. Leave you cold. At least, that had been my experience. 'You may be right,' he replied thoughtfully. 'Anyway, tonight I'll try it your way. No costume. No funny walk. Heaven knows I can't die a worse death than I did tonight!'

Great man that he is, he took my advice and to my delight all the laughs were coming in the right places and he finished to a standing ovation. After the curtain came down he rushed back to the dressing-room and embraced me with tears in his eyes. 'What a clever pusskin you are, Mike!' he cried.

While on the Rock I got to know that popular member of our little company, whose comic song 'Wind around my Heart' was also more or less her signature tune, Beatrice Lillie. No one would ever have guessed, watching her gagging her way through her act, that her heart was broken. Three months before her only son had been reported missing after a German torpedo struck his ship in the Atlantic. She confided in me her steadfast belief that her son was safe and that it would be only a matter of time before he was traced.

I noticed that after performances for the Navy, when the lads crowded onto the stage to shake hands with the cast, Bea always asked them if they had known her son or had news of him. One night, she found herself shaking hands with a young midshipman who had served on her son's ship. She broke down in tears. 'You have survived,' she cried, 'surely there is some hope for my son? Tell me exactly what happened.' Embarrassed, the midshipman mumbled 'It all happened so quickly, Ma'am. He was the last man to leave the ship. He stayed at his post until the rest of us were safe on life-rafts. He was a very brave man, Ma'am.' Bea smiled through her tears 'Thank you for saying that. Somehow it makes it easier.'

Noel Coward told me how she came to terms with her loss. She had been among his guests at a house-party given to celebrate the first armistice. 'We watched from a balcony overlooking the Cenotaph,' he told me. 'After the king had laid his wreath and the Last Post had been sounded, Bea plucked the single poppy from her lapel and dropped it down into the street. It is my guess that in that moment she finally said farewell to her son.'

After my return from Gib my personal life resumed the same aimless pattern. I fell in and out of love, or something like it, with monotonous regularity. But I never met anyone important enough for me to think about asking Kay for a divorce. No. I lie. There was one exception – a love affair that came to an abrupt and galling finale.

The object of my passion was the actress Sally Gray, who possessed the beauty of a traditional English rose combined with the sex appeal of Jean Harlow. We met while making a film which was such a flop that I don't even remember the title. To my mind, Sally never made the impact she deserved because her beauty seemed to debar her in film producers' minds from also having brains.

I was completely smitten. But apart from allowing me to escort her to first nights and take her out to dinner from time to time she kept me at arm's length. One night, after an evening's dancing at Ciro's, she allowed me to kiss her goodnight. But as usual I was not invited past the door. Frustrated, I stood gazing up at the window of her second-floor flat, like some lovelorn youth, then suddenly my eye lighted on a notice-board on the front of the building saying 'Flat to Let'.

The following morning, without a word to Sally, I whipped round to the estate agent's, took the flat and moved in the same day. Next time I called for her I went down and rang the door-bell as if I had come in from the street. Then the inevitable happened. One evening about midnight we met head-on in the middle of the stairs. Sally was livid when I explained that I had become her neighbour. 'How dare you follow me around like a detective?' she demanded. 'Because I adore you,' I replied. 'All right,' she retorted, white with anger, 'but don't say I didn't warn you.'

Taking my arm, she led me up one flight to her front door, turned the key in the lock and with a mock bow ushered me inside. It was then I heard it - a voice coming from the bedroom singing a very out-of-tune version of *'These Foolish Things'*. Next moment a tall, good-looking young man dressed in the uniform of a major walked out of the bedroom. Smiling serenely, Sally turned to me and said, simply, 'Mike, meet my fiancé.'

So ended a romance that never was. You might think a thwarted love affair would have had the effect of channelling all my energies into work; but it didn't, although there was no shortage of jobs. My agent said 'I just wish I could cut you in half, Mike, then you could take all the parts you are being offered!' I should have been spurred on by the increasing interest I was beginning to attract in the press. Elspeth Grant wrote in the *Daily Graphic*: 'Wilding is an actor just waiting for the right break. I only hope he has the sense, when it comes, to grab it with both hands. But on meeting the young man, I found him overwhelmingly modest and singularly lacking in ambition.'

How right she was. I have used the word 'jobbing' to head this chapter because that is exactly how I approached my career at that time - moving from job to job like a bricklayer, without any yearning to work on something larger or more inspiring. If ever an actor needed a guiding hand, an interpreter, a prophet, a mentor, then that actor was me and by the most happy and memorable accident of my life I was soon to meet such a man. His name was Herbert Wilcox.

7
Star by Default

IT all began on a quiet Sunday afternoon in 1943. Herbert Wilcox and his wife, Anna Neagle, lived in Elstree and during weekends went on long country walks. In his autobiography *Twenty-five Thousand Sunsets* Herbert relates how on one of these outings they met a neighbour, Maurice Cowan, then editor of *Picturegoer*. Maurice said casually 'I've got a good subject for you', and he outlined the story of *I Live in Grosvenor Square*. To which Herbert replied 'Say no more, it's mine.' It was to be the first of the successful 'London series'.

In *I Live in Grosvenor Square* Herbert co-starred Anna with Rex Harrison and the result was such a smash hit both with the press and public that Herbert planned to continue the partnership in his next film. But alas for Herbert, because of his performance in *Grosvenor Square*, Hollywood snapped up Rex Harrison with a long-term contract. His next choice was John Mills, but Mills was not available. Several other star names were considered, including James Mason and Stewart Granger, but Herbert was unsure whether either was right for the part or whether either would be such a perfect foil for Anna.

I had just found a new agent, Eric Goodhead, a fine, sensitive man in whom I had complete trust. Goodhead's persistence was rewarded. 'Wilcox is desperate,' Eric told me over the phone, 'so he has agreed to look at one of your film clips.'

Well, I thought to myself, desperate film producers sometimes resort to desperate measures. I didn't put my chances any higher than that, though I cheered up a little when Eric told me that the film clip he'd chosen was taken from the film *Dear Octopus*, in which I had taken over the role played by Gielgud on the stage. The high spot – and one that petrified me on the set – was a five-minute after-dinner speech in which, as the youngest member of a noble family, I had to explain the 'tentacles' of affection which gave the piece its title. I got through it without a fluff and was most touched when the cast, which included Marie Lohr, Margaret Lockwood and Sybil Thorndike, broke into spontaneous applause.

By arrangement with Eric I waited until the lights went down, then slipped into a back seat in the projection theatre. The clip had just started and there I was in full flow, when suddenly the sound broke down. The only impression Anna and Herbert must have received was that of a young man opening and shutting his mouth like a goldfish and waving his arms about like a politician.

When the lights went up no one said a word. I wished the floor would open and swallow me – and I was about to rush out of the theatre when Eric called me back and made the introductions, which I went through in a daze. I remember Herbert saying 'Better luck next time' and Anna's sympathetic smile as she murmured 'What very bad luck.' Then I fled out of the theatre.

Arriving back at my flat half an hour later, I mixed myself a bumper-sized drink, collapsed in a chair and said to myself 'Goodbye, Herbert Wilcox.' Then the phone rang. To my astonishment it was Herbert, whose first words were 'Will you have dinner with Anna and me at Claridges tonight?' I arrived shaking so violently that Herbert, filling my glass for the third time, said 'Have some more champers. Good for the nerves.' But the more I drank the more tongue-tied I became.

Twenty-five years later, I read Herbert's impressions of that evening: 'We found him charming, delightful, diffident, but was this enough? . . . Since there was absolutely no alternative and the film was due to commence in a few days, in desperation I signed Wilding, but with many misgivings.'

Next day, Eric called. 'You've got the part,' he said. 'I'm sending you round a copy of the script with Herbert's compliments. The rest is up to you. Kiss your nerves goodbye. With Wilcox at the helm, I'm sure you'll be a great success.' 'I only wish I had your confidence,' I replied. 'Wish me luck, I'm going to need it.'

The title of the film was *Piccadilly Incident*. It was a dramatic subject with overtones of tragedy. Briefly, it was the story of an encounter between two people during a London air raid who fall in love and get married. But Diana (Anna) as a Wren is ordered overseas directly after the wedding. Her ship is torpedoed and the few survivors, Diana among them, find themselves marooned on a desert island. Eventually, they are rescued and Diana returns to London to learn that her husband (me) is married to another girl and has a young baby. They meet again and discover that they are still in love. The solution to this unhappy triangle is a tragic one. Diana is killed in an air raid.

Now here was a role which called for strong dramatic acting unlike anything I had ever done before. I arrived for the first day's shooting a bundle of nerves. First, I met the chief make-up man, Fletch. I was sitting in the make-up chair trying to appear calm when Fletch remarked jokingly 'You have got a big face, haven't you?' 'Have I?' I asked, 'I've never thought about it before.' 'Acres of it,' said Fletch, breathing heavily as he rubbed in the grease-paint. 'Like a horse?' I suggested. 'Yes,' agreed Fletch, laughing, 'just like a horse.' So I went on the set feeling like an unwanted big-faced horse.

Herbert's and Anna's feelings on that first day matched my own uncertainty. 'Then, on the second day,' Anna recalls in *There's Always Tomorrow*, 'something very strange happened. In a not particularly important scene,

Michael performed some instinctive piece of "business" which made me blink and mentally sit up. That evening I said to Herbert. "Do you think he is as good as I do?" "Better," he replied. "Here's one leading man I am not going to lose to Hollywood." '

The last day of that picture brought one of the most exhilarating moments of my career. I was sitting studying my lines when Herbert walked up to me, gently took the script from me and thrust a piece of paper under my nose. 'Could you put up with me as your director for the next ten years?' he demanded. 'If so, put your moniker on this contract.' Thus began the six happiest and most successful years of my career.

To this day, I don't know why Anna and I made such perfect partners. *'Piccadilly Incident'*, wrote Anna, 'was rather a sad story, but it had a sort of magic about it; and two of the ingredients of the magic were Michael and me. We just welded. Our chemistry was right.' Happily this reaction was reflected by the critics. One, Godfrey Winn, wrote: 'In the film *Piccadilly Incident* is born the greatest team in British films.'

In addition, there was a personal harmony between us that was almost uncanny. My sense of the ridiculous was matched by Herbert's wit and Anna was an appreciative audience of both. However, although she had been kindness itself, as completely unselfish off the set as on it, I still sensed in her manner something I could not quite understand. Then one morning during a break in shooting Anna leant over and touched my arm and, gazing at me wistfully, said 'There is something you must know about me. Something awful. I am afraid I have no sense of humour.' Who in the world but Anna would have made such a confession? In fact, it wasn't true. About a week later she gave me a still showing us surrounded by a group of luscious chorus girls. I was clearly oblivious of the photo being taken and instead of gazing into Anna's eyes I was ogling the chorus girls. Anna had written across the bottom of the still, 'How is this for a green-eyed Neagle?'

Herbert was a born raconteur and Anna so adored him that she was content to play audience. Come to that, I have found that most female artists noted for their sense of humour derive their wit from catty stories about other players. But whenever I tried to tell Anna a catty joke she would put her hands over her ears and cry 'Stop! I don't want to hear it.'

In fact I soon learned never to pull her leg about her profession. If I made a joking reference to how she played a certain scene, her face would fall and she would implore 'I wasn't really that bad, was I?' She was the most totally dedicated actress I have ever met and Herbert told me that Anna had once mentioned to him that, like Peg Woffington, she hoped to die on the stage.

Herbert lost no time in cashing in on our first success. Our next picture was *The Courtneys of Curzon Street*. The story had a touch of *Cavalcade* about it, inasmuch as it traced the history of one house and one family from the beginning of the century to the blitz. My role was again a dramatic one, including a new departure for me since it called for a transformation from youth to old age.

The make-up department's first efforts at making me look seventy were a flop. I wore a fuzzy white wig and lines were drawn on my face, but the final result made me look like Santa Claus. Finally, Herbert called in Guy Pierce, a Hollywood make-up genius. His technique was to fit a thin gauze mask over the actor's own face, then take it away to his workshop and, using putty and grease-paint, mould the contours of an ageing face directly onto the mask.

The result was amazing and a little chilling, for I saw reflected in the mirror a preview of how I might look thirty years on. I still had to master the faltering movements of an old man, which is not as easy as it sounds. I wish I had known then a trick David Niven told me about many years later when we met in Hollywood. In *Enchantment*, when he had to act a seventy-year-old, he had two pounds of lead put into the sole of each shoe to take the spring out of his step.

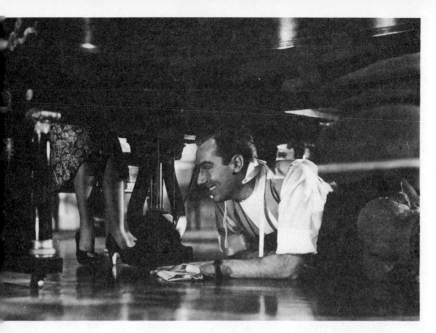

19   *Spring in Park Lane* – what the butler saw! Me admiring Anna's ankles.

20   *Spring in Park Lane* – with Peter Graves between scenes.

21 *Spring in Park Lane* – romance over the washing up

22 *Spring in Park Lane* – a picnic in the park

23   *Spring in Park Lane* – love blossoms at last

24 Tom Walls, Anna, Herbert and myself during the filming of *Spring in Park Lane*

25 *Spring in Park Lane* – Herbert, Anna and myself relaxing between takes

26 *Spring in Park Lane* – Anna and I stepping out in the dream
dance scene

27   Being interviewed for 'In Town Tonight', following the success of *Spring in Park Lane*

28   Anna, Herbert and myself clutching our *Daily Mail* awards

29 *Maytime in Mayfair* – manager and boss of a fashionable dress shop

0 *Maytime in Mayfair* – manager and boss get together for some late night igh jinks

31 Trying out a jok
on Nick Phipps
between scenes, whi
shooting *Maytime in
Mayfair*

32 *Under Capricorn* -
me as the English
visitor, trying to
persuade Ingrid
Bergman she can
overcome her drink
problem

33 Learning from Hitch during the filming of *Under Capricorn*

34 *Under Capricorn* – sharing a laugh with Joseph Cotten

35   My goddess

The Courtneys was an even greater success than *Piccadilly* and to my surprise I found myself in great demand not only in England, but in Hollywood too. But Herbert turned down all bids from Hollywood, saying 'Even if the parts were right, which they are not, I can't see you feeling at home in that slave market.'

However, an offer from Korda to play a leading role in *An Ideal Husband* was a different matter. 'Working for Korda can only add to your film education,' said Herbert; and as for me, I considered the offer a great compliment. Alas, a few minutes' explanation from my agent and I soon came down to earth. He told me that Korda had lost his first choice for the role in *An Ideal Husband* when Rex Harrison had been called up and he was willing to test me for the part. I have been nominated as second choice to Harrison at least three times. He has haunted me like a spectre down the years, finally reappearing while I was living and working in Hollywood, when an American stage producer offered me Rex's role in a touring version of *My Fair Lady*. I turned it down flat on the grounds that I could not sing. 'Neither could Rex,' replied the producer, 'but he learned.' 'What makes you think I can do what Rex can do?' I demanded furiously. I still think I made the right decision. Rex has made Professor Higgins his own unique creation.

But to return to Korda, what a charmer that man was! At our very first meeting he paid me a compliment which I treasured. 'Dear boy,' he smiled, 'after you walked into the room I put all ideas of a test out of my mind. You were born to play the part. Oscar Wilde's hero come to life!' During the making of *Ideal Husband* I met two enchanting actresses. The one, Paulette Goddard, I found so irresistible that I joined the queue of her admirers and dated her whenever I could. The other, Diana Wynyard, had such a queenly air about her that I felt quite overawed and blew my lines in our first scene together, not once but three times. I was so furious with myself that I let out a French obscenity. You can imagine my chagrin when such a madonna-like creature countered, also in French, with something equally rude. She made it clear she was swearing with me, not at me, and we soon became great friends.

Korda also spoke, among many languages, perfect French – but there were few things at which Korda was not a master. I have never met anyone who could do so much so perfectly all at the same time. While directing *Ideal Husband*, he would be   na *Karenina* between shots,   xt production. At the same   ηy Kimmins would dart in a   ut shooting *Mine Own Execu*   ;o producing. Not content w   ιs going on in his head at t   n during lunch break he cou   g catalogues of rare books, ᴏ ᴡʜɪᴄʜ ne was a fervent collector.

He worked an eighteen-hour day, utterly ignoring his indifferent state of health. Once he collapsed on the set and a doctor was called, who diagnosed a mild heart attack, saying 'Unless you have absolute rest, Sir Alex, I cannot answer for the consequences.' 'Nonsense,' retorted Korda, 'I'm just a little tired, that's all,' and he returned to the set and finished the day's work, afterwards presiding at a party to celebrate the last day's shooting.

By the time I worked for him Korda was already a legend, regarded not only as a film genius but as a financial wizard. How he staved off bankruptcy in the early part of his career has become a part of British film history. Since he was already up to his neck in debt, his creditors not only refused him further money to continue his next production but threatened him with bankruptcy. He arrived at the meeting of his angry bankers in a Rolls he had not paid for, wearing an impeccable Savile Row suit made by well-known tailors who were daily issuing writs for settlement of his account, like all his other personal accounts, long overdue. The press had turned up in force to report on what looked like being the great man's darkest hour. However, when pestered for his comment, Korda quipped 'You should never ask a man who is facing bankruptcy any questions about his feelings. Wait until he has faced the ordeal and overcome it as I intend to do.'

The meeting was like the famous scene in *If I Had a Million* when Charles Laughton thumbs his nose at his boss. Korda had faced his creditors owing about £200,000. He ended the day not only having fobbed off their requests for payment but also having wheedled out of them a loan of more than twice that sum. When asked about this coup, Korda replied 'Inside every banker, even the governor of the Bank of England, there lies a gambling streak. In me, they recognise one of their own kind.'

In 1942 he was given a knighthood. When I happened to meet him a few days later and congratulated him, he smiled and said 'Now, even if I cannot pronounce the language correctly, I feel like a bona fide Englishman!' – and added that the proudest moment of his life had been when Churchill asked for a private viewing of his film *Lady Hamilton*, starring Vivien Leigh and Laurence Olivier. At the end of the film, when the lights went up in his private projection room in the bowels of the War Office, Churchill turned to Korda with tears in his eyes. 'Whenever I feel my spirits are at a low ebb,' he said, 'I shall send for your film. You have made an epic on seeing which every Englishman will feel renewed pride in belonging to our island race.'

When I returned to the Wilcox–Neagle fold Herbert was pondering over a subject for our next film. Then he had a brainwave. In the thirties he had made a comedy with Jack Buchanan based on a book by Alice Duer Miller called *Come Out of the Pantry*. (In retrospect, the story contained several ingredients of the TV success *Upstairs, Downstairs*.) But he was worried that as it stood it was primarily a comedy exercise. 'Why should that be a drawback?' I asked him. 'After all, comedy has been my forte at Ealing.' 'That's in the past,' replied Herbert, 'I have launched you in the romantic image in the public mind. That's what your fans are after, romance.'

So with the help of screenwriter Nicholas Phipps, Herbert completely transformed the story – and as soon as I read it I knew they had handed me my best role to date. Once again Herbert plumped for a London place-name for the title: even after all these years it still stands as my trade-mark, *Spring in Park Lane*.

But *Spring* did not get off to a happy beginning, at least so far as I was concerned. I had flown over to join Herbert and Anna at a little seaside resort near Dublin, where ostensibly they were taking a short holiday: in reality Herbert was writing the script.

During the shooting of *The Courtneys* I had watched Anna dancing and was so impressed with her grace that when the scene ended I impulsively picked her up and swung her round in a 'cartwheel lift'. 'Why, you can dance!' exclaimed Anna in surprise. I explained that such talent as I might have had was limited to my days in rep. But Anna as well as being sweet is also very shrewd, as I discovered on my first evening with them in Ireland.

We were served a sumptuous dinner. There was still food rationing in England and here we were all three of us sitting down to enormous mouth-watering Irish steaks. I was just tucking in when Anna said in her innocent but straightforward way 'Herbert, have you told Michael about the dance?'

I choked on my steak. 'What dance?' I demanded. 'Get on with your steak, Mike, before it gets cold,' said Herbert. I exploded. 'I'm not eating another mouthful till you tell me what this is about!'

Herbert, seeing there was nothing else for it, grudgingly admitted that he had written in a dance sequence for Anna and me to perform. I replied flatly 'I can't do it, Herbert. And that's that. I'm not going to make an idiot of myself.' As always, Herbert was not going to take no for an answer. 'Calm down,' he said soothingly and went on to explain, 'I see it as a dream sequence and it will be shot in slow motion.' Now, I had seen films of boxing in slow motion and even when falling on their backsides the participants seemed to do so with a certain grace. I put this comparison to Herbert. 'Exactly,' he said, 'even if you fall on your face, you'll look graceful.'

As it turned out, the dream dance was one of the high spots of the film. But learning the routine would have been a nightmare had it not been for the patient instruction given to me by Philip and Betty Buchel. The critics reacted as if I had been a song-and-dance man all my life. But on the first night, a young woman came up to me for my autograph and asked 'You didn't really do that dance yourself, did you?' I can only imagine that she had seen Larry Parks in *The Jolson Story*.

Spring played to packed audiences all over the country, even being shown at two Leicester Square cinemas at the same time for a while during its second year, and the culminating triumph came when the *Daily Mail* gave each of us an award – as the best producer, actress and actor of the year. To this day its box-office record has never been beaten, not even by *The Sound of Music*.

Spring was still running when Herbert announced his plan to cash in on our success with a similar romantic comedy. The story, scripted by Nicholas Phipps from Herbert's basic idea, was of a lord (me) who owns a Mayfair dress shop and the manageress (Anna) with whom he inevitably falls in love. Nick, a brilliant lyric writer who had achieved fame with the revue *Sweet and Low*, became one of my closest friends. He was everyone's idea of a foppish Englishman and Herbert asked him to play the Marquis of Borechester in *Spring* and Sir Henry Hazelrigg in *Maytime*, parts which he performed to perfection. Peter Graves, the son of Lord Tommy Graves, also appeared in both films and became a lifelong friend. The three of us larked like schoolboys on the set, disrupting shooting so often that Herbert nicknamed us

'The Three Musketeers'. *Maytime in Mayfair* was a frothy bit of nonsense, but the audience loved it and Reg Whitley, film critic of the *Daily Mirror*, wrote: 'This happy trio have done it again. Here is a film which stands up to the entertainment standards set by *Spring in Park Lane* and that's saying something.'

But Herbert still held out against the increasing barrage of Hollywood requests. 'Wait until they come up with the right subject' was his advice. 'So far no one has made an offer worthy of your talents.'

However, when a man whom I considered to be a genius joined the queue, at first I didn't take the proposal seriously. I said to Herbert, 'Surely he must have got me mixed up with some other actor?' 'A man like Hitch never gets mixed up about actors or anything else,' retorted Herbert. 'Mark my words, you will be hearing from him sooner than you think.' Sure enough, he had barely left the flat five minutes when the phone rang. A nasal voice with a slight trace of Cockney drawled, 'May I speak to Mr Michael Wilding?' 'Speaking,' I replied. 'Allow me to introduce myself,' the drawling voice continued. 'My name is Alfred Hitchcock. How would you like to try working with me?'

A week later I flew out to New York for my first conference with him. He had a lavish suite at the St Regis Hotel and after we had shaken hands and ordered drinks I expected him to get straight down to the business of the film. Not a bit of it. 'Do you know New York well?' he inquired. I replied that this was my first visit. 'Oh,' said Hitch, 'we must remedy that.' I doubt if many natives of the city could equal Hitch's knowledge; certainly no one could have given me such a guided tour, which took in everything from Harlem to the Empire State Building. We ended our trip by taking the ferry from Staten Island. As we passed the Statue of Liberty, Hitch handed me his field-glasses. 'Take a look at the lady's anatomy,' he drawled, 'can't you guess that a Frenchman had a hand in constructing those bosoms?'

Well, much as I enjoyed his company and his jokes, after three days I began to wonder when he would bring up the subject of the film or, even more important, open up about his attitudes to film-making. But he did let one remark slip about his approach to directing: 'The secret of suspense in a film,' he told me, 'is never to begin a scene at the beginning and never let it go on to the end.'

But apart from that telling remark he refused to be drawn. So I went to see an old American pal, the brilliant film historian at the New York Museum of Modern Art, Richard Griffith. He thrust into my hands a copy of an American film magazine in which Hitch contributed a detailed analysis of his system of working. 'Take that away with you,' said Dick. 'I think it will give you some of the answers.'

Two sentences in the article I still remember: 'If you start a picture with a man coming into a room through a door,' Hitch had written, 'that's ordinary. If you show him coming in through a window, that's extraordinary. My definition of true suspense is when the ordinary meets the extraordinary.'

My first film for Hitch, *Under Capricorn,* co-starred Ingrid Bergman and Joseph Cotten. Also in the cast was Margaret Leighton. Strange that the woman who one day was to bring me the greatest happiness of my life should have made so insignificant a first impression. I recognised her obvious talents as an actress, but thought of her as a rather toffee-nosed member of the Old Vic – and, while she respected Joe Cotten because of his background in the famous New York Mercury Theatre, she seemed to regard me as a mere flash-in-the-pan movie ham. At any rate, she never offered me more than somewhat frigid politeness; and even if she had I don't suppose I would have been impressed, since at the time I was walking out with Ingrid Bergman.

I had always imagined that Bergman was as cold and aloof as a statue on a pedestal. So I was surprised and delighted with her ever-present sense of humour, sometimes wicked, always witty. We had a lot of fun together on and off the set. Worried about mastering an Irish brogue, after hearing me tell some of my Cockney jokes she said one day 'You seem to have a flair for accents. Will you give me some lessons?'

I was more than a little smitten by Bergman and this was the excuse I had been waiting for to ask her out to dinner and back to my flat afterwards for some Irish tuition. I fear my efforts in that direction were not very successful. I saw the film again recently on television and we certainly made a strange-sounding trio – Joe with his American accent, my own clipped English and Ingrid's Swedish-Irish. As the shooting progressed Ingrid gave up and slipped back into her normal accent, which was so strong I sometimes had difficulty in understanding her and used to tease here by imitating her vowels. But she took my kidding in good part and after the film was finished sent me a photo of herself signed 'To my dear old friendt'.

As for Joe Cotten, for the first couple of days' shooting we sniffed at each other like suspicious dogs until we found that we both laughed at the same things, and we have been great friends ever since. Joe rechristened the picture 'Under Crapricorn', which I don't think amused Hitch too much.

But as for Hitch's qualities as a director, a kinder, gentler man never stood behind the camera. Hitch, however, wasn't always behind the camera; he projected his bulk above, below, behind, in front of it, or often directly in its path. He had this bug about 'ten-minute takes'. Just coping with the sets would have floored most directors. Walls parted and we acted with miles of cable underfoot so that the camera could travel through three or four sets in one take. All the sound was dubbed in afterwards and during scenes Hitch would shout directions to his cameramen like the captain of a fishing fleet exhorting his crew to pull in the nets.

On one occasion while Ingrid and I were in the middle

of a passionate love scene Hitch let out a howl of pain, then in the most gentle tone said 'Please move the camera a little to the right. You have just run over my foot.' The X-ray revealed later that the camera's weight had broken his big toe, but he was much too much of a gentleman to swear in front of ladies.

Hitch did not often throw compliments around, but at the end of a difficult scene, if an actress was involved, he would walk up to her and kiss her hand. If it was an actor, he would slap him on the back and murmur 'Bully for you, old bean!' That is why I recall so well a compliment he paid to me during the shooting of *Under Capricorn*. The scene really belonged to Bergman. She had to recount the tragic story of her life while I just sat there and listened. At the end of the scene Hitch walked over to me and said 'Bully for you, old bean. You can listen. Most actors either sit as expressionless as stuffed dummies or over-react in an attempt to steal the scene. But you, Mike, are that rare thing, a born listener.'

My admiration for Hitch's genius is unbounded, so you can imagine my delight when as soon as we had finished *Capricorn* he asked me to play in *Stage Fright*, which proved to be a landmark in both my private and my professional life, for it gave me the chance to meet Marlene Dietrich. Before our meeting, Hitch summed up his own opinion of her. 'Marlene', he said, 'is more than just a superb professional actress. She is also a professional cameraman, director, editor, make-up artist, composer, producer. In all these arts she is a supreme master.'

There was something quite magnetic about Marlene – for, as Charles Higham wrote in his biography of her: 'What other woman could list Erich Maria Remarque, Maurice Chevalier, Jean Gabin, Fritz Lang, Joseph von Sternberg, Mike Todd, James Stewart, Willi Forst, Douglas Fairbanks Junior, Brian Aherne, John Gilbert, John Wayne and Yul Brynner among the men who loved her?'

My first sight of Marlene was breathtaking. She was

lying on a sofa, draped in furs, her lovely legs gleaming in black tights, looking like a twentieth-century Venus. Hitch was running behind schedule, so we were hustled straight into our first scene together. At the end of the scene, in which I spoke only twice, Dietrich turned to Hitch and said 'Why don't you give this young man more lines?' At her suggestion my role was greatly enlarged and, without being the least bit patronising, she started giving me helpful suggestions, which brought out the best in me. Naturally I was grateful, but by the end of the first week's shooting my feelings for her went far beyond gratitude. I was completely bewitched and tongue-tied – and would have remained thus, had not Marlene broken the silence herself.

It happened almost by accident. Marlene's car had broken down, so when we finished filming I offered her a lift. It was bitterly cold after the previous night's snowfall and as we drove through Hyde Park we saw some children having a snowball fight. 'Oh!' cried Marlene, 'let's stop and join them! I haven't had a snowball battle since I was a little girl in Berlin!' I stopped the car and we joined in the kids' game, chucking snowballs at each other. Suddenly, Marlene slipped on the ice and literally fell into my arms. She looked up at me and said 'I wish I had met you when I was that little girl in Berlin. Now I am old. Too old for you.' I replied 'Shakespeare said it for me "Age cannot wither her, nor custom stale . . ."' I broke off. 'I'm sorry, I can't remember the rest of it.' 'Then why not just settle for kissing me?' she said.

From that moment we became inseparable. Gossip started in the studio when she began to arrive for work in my Rolls-Royce. We went to theatres, night clubs, first nights, in fact everywhere around town together. Inevitably the press started to hound us and, in the absence of co-operation from either of us, began to churn out lurid accounts of our relationship. I was furious, but Marlene took it all serenely. She simply smiled her enigmatic smile and murmured 'Whoever said publish and be damned was speaking for me – for us!'

To me it seemed a miracle. How could such a goddess find the ideal companion in me? But she did. In fact she would not move a step without me. She insisted that I accompany her everywhere – to her hairdresser, her dressmaker, even to the beauty parlour – and asked me what I felt about how she looked, how she did her hair, what she wore, which perfume I preferred. And she took as much interest in my appearance as she did in her own. She accompanied me to my tailor, helped me pick the right material, commented on the cut, chose my ties and even my socks. She also persuaded me to find a decent barber's, after years of going to the nearest and cheapest, which she scornfully dismissed as 'pudding-basin butchers'. 'You have a romantic head, like Byron's,' she said. 'You should have a romantic haircut too.'

But, close as we became, there was an unfathomable quality about Marlene, a part of her that remained aloof. Every time a fresh glimpse of her personality was revealed, I felt there were still further depths beyond my reach. That was her magic, her secret, her mystery. Sadly our relationship came to an abrupt end – and yet, although thirty years have passed since our parting, whenever I think of her I do so not only with lasting affection, but with a deep sense of awe that such a magical being ever gave me the time of day.

I also take comfort in the added miracle that she apparently still holds me in her affections. Only three years ago when I was in hospital and reported as dying, she sent me a cable saying 'DEAR MIKE, DON'T DIE YET. IT'S MY TURN FIRST.' When I read it I wept, for it proved that in addition to all her other qualities she possessed a forgiving heart.

8
Life at the Top

BY now Herbert had made a major decision about my future. 'The time has come for you to make your Hollywood début,' he said. 'That way you will become an international name.' After much thought and insisting on veto rights over the script, he agreed to loan me to Warner Brothers to appear in a film with Greer Garson called *The Law and the Lady*. The story concerned an ambitious lady's maid of the Victorian era who set up in business as a crook with the black sheep of a noble family. Only two things went wrong with my first Hollywood venture. First, the script was a complete rewrite from the version approved by Herbert; secondly, it turned out to be a lousy movie. I was given impossible lines to speak and Greer, equally unhappy for the same reason, tried to inject some humour into her role by attempting a Cockney accent. I saw the film again recently and the only funny thing about it, apart from my own lamentable performance, was Greer's concept of Cockney speech.

My first and most lasting impression of Hollywood was that of living in a cell and working in a factory. The cell was a luxurious, chromium-plated apartment in a Beverly Hills hotel, equipped with some rather surprising mod cons, including four gold telephones and a mirror-walled bathroom which boasted a gold bidet and four taps marked 'hot', 'cold', 'iced', and 'orange juice'.

The factory was Warner Brothers' studio. I arrived

outside the locked iron gates at 6 a.m. for my first morning's work only to be stopped by a gateman with a gun on his hip and an accent straight from the Mafia, who demanded to see my pass. When I said I had no pass, he shook his head. 'Nobody gets past these gates without a pass.' 'Call the director,' I said. 'He'll know who I am.' The gateman looked at me as if I was an idiot. 'Directors don't arrive till eight o'clock.' 'Then call Mr Warner's office,' I said. 'Mr Warner don't git in before eleven o'clock.'

Instead of being angry, I laughed. 'Do you realise I've travelled 6,000 miles at Mr Warner's expense, and here are you refusing to let me drive the last 600 yards through your goddam gates?' 'No pass, no admittance,' came the surly reply. To add insult to injury, when two hours later the director arrived it took me five minutes to convince him that I was a bona fide member of the cast.

By the time I had got my make-up on I made my first appearance on the set an hour late, to be introduced to an obviously annoyed Miss Garson. 'I hope unpunctuality is not a habit with you Mr Wilder?' she inquired icily. 'The name's Wilding,' I murmured, but she continued to call me Mr Wilder throughout the shooting. Come the lunch break, Miss Garson disappeared into her dressing-room, the director disappeared for an appointment with the boss and I had to find my own way to the studio restaurant, which was crowded with famous faces. Feeling like an interloper, I slunk to a corner table. A waitress, who could have doubled for Betty Grable, asked me for my order. 'I'll start with a double Scotch, please,' I said. I might as well have asked for cyanide, judging by the look on her face. 'No alcoholic drinks served here,' she said. 'By whose order?' I asked. She gave me a look of utter scorn. 'Mr Warner's orders, of course.' So I settled for a glass of buttermilk and a Warners' Weiner Salad. During the next few weeks of solitary liquorless lunches I ran through 'Stanwyck Stew', 'Cooper Casserole' and 'Robinson's Risotto', all equally tasteless and the latter so tough that the chief ingredient might have been Edward G.'s toes.

At six o'clock I would drive back to my luxury cell, mix myself a double Scotch and turn on the television, not so much to watch it, for I soon found the programmes infinitely boring, but just for the company. Then I would learn my lines for the following day and at ten o'clock retire to bed. I have never spent such a monastic six weeks in my life. I realised that so far as Hollywood was concerned I was a nobody. I hadn't expected to be besieged by invitations, but I thought I might have merited a friendly nod from the British set or an invitation from my boss. But, strange as it may seem, I never set eyes on Jack Warner, let alone had a drink with him.

My arrival back in England coincided with the ill-fated London première of *The Law and the Lady*, which despite pleas from the studio press officer I refused to attend. Loyal as ever, Herbert and Anna went along. Next morning at nine o'clock my door bell rang. I staggered out of bed to find Herbert standing on the doorstep with a bundle of newspapers under his arm, which he handed me, beaming. 'Your press notices,' he said. I groaned. 'It was a stinker, wasn't it? There's no need to rub my nose in it.' 'How's this for a lousy review?' said Herbert, and, opening the *Daily Express*, he thrust it under my nose. The headline jumped out at me: 'CHAMPAGNE FOR MR WILDING!' Herbert said 'Leonard Mosley pans the film, but listen to what he has to say about you. "Despite mediocre material, Mr Wilding carries the Union Jack right into the heart of Hollywood. He is truly an international star."'

Today, a quarter of a century later, people often ask me what it was like to be a top star. At the time I just couldn't take it seriously; I thought my success was a flash in the pan. I had always regarded myself as a nonsense actor with a bit of a flair for comedy, who had been lucky enough to become Anna Neagle's leading man. My diffidence about my success must have been infuriating to Herbert. Indeed, with his usual Irish stubbornness he set out to prove the point.

Spring had just received the *Daily Mail* award for the best film of the year. The following Sunday Herbert put his 'plot' into operation, under the guise of a casual invitation to their weekend flat in Brighton. I had no idea Herbert had arranged that Anna and I should make an appearance at a cinema in Worthing, where *Spring* was opening. The first inkling I had that something was afoot was when after lunch an enormous limousine drew up outside the front door.

'We're taking you for a ride, Mike,' announced Herbert, pushing me into the back. Then I noticed that we had a police escort. 'Herbert,' I shouted, 'what are you doing to me?' 'Opening your eyes, I hope,' replied Herbert cheerfully.

Before we reached Worthing, it had begun to drizzle, but hundreds of people were lining the pavements on either side of the road and cheering as we passed. By the time we reached the theatre it was pouring, but there must have been close on a thousand people waiting to see us arrive. The theatre manager came out armed with umbrellas and, with the help of two commissionaires, pushed a path for us through the crowd. In the cinema, after the film was over, Herbert strode onto the stage to the accompaniment of a fanfare from the orchestra. He introduced Anna, who also got a fanfare, then she went into her dance. On cue I joined her. When we had finished dancing, meaning it as a joke, I said 'Herbert got a fanfare. Anna got a fanfare. How about a fanfare for me?' The leader of the orchestra took me seriously. 'Just walk off and walk on again, Mr Wilding, and we will give you a fanfare.' So I walked off and walked on again, this time to a terrific fanfare, to which I replied with an imitation of a Groucho Marx walk. 'Thanks,' I said, 'I've never had a fanfare before in my life and I don't suppose I ever will again.' The audience rose to their feet shouting 'Encore!' So I walked off and on again and again, asking 'Can I do it again?'

'Yes!' chorused the audience in one voice. So I repeated the routine and this time the band struck up 'Auld Lang Syne' and the audience, who had completely joined in the joke, took up the chorus. That was the first and last fanfare I ever had and I must admit I enjoyed every minute of it.

Next time Herbert ordered me to savour an audience's response it was rather different. *Spring* had just opened at the Empire in Brixton and Herbert said to me 'It's one thing to go over big in the West End. But it's time you learned the reaction of the other three-quarters of your audience.'

So I hired a taxi and made my way to Brixton. As we drove along, I noticed how shabby the people looked, how dilapidated their houses, how drab their surroundings.

At last the taxi pulled up outside the cinema and, disguised by dark glasses and with my hat pulled over my eyes, I joined the queue. Obeying Herbert's instructions, I bought the cheapest seat and slunk into the first empty hole in the one-and-ninepennies. The picture was midway through and I found myself sitting next to a very large lady intent on devouring a bag of fish and chips as if she hadn't eaten for a week. Every time I appeared on the screen she rustled her chip-bag and announced in a voice that could be heard all over the cinema 'Wot an 'orrible 'at! Fancy wearing such an 'orrible 'at!'

Now the offending hat was a snapped-brimmed trilby which I wore on and off the screen and which had practically become my trademark. In fact, hats have always been a hobby of mine. I collect them in all shapes and sizes, from sailor caps to cowboy sombreros. As the lights came up, I discarded the trilby, donned my dark glasses and slunk out of the cinema. When I got back home I phoned Herbert and said 'If ever you find me being halfway pleased with what I've done, just remind me of that Cockney voice screaming about my 'orrible 'at!'

On New Year's Eve Herbert invited me to his Park Lane flat for a drink and a chat about my future. He started off by saying 'Mike, after four years' non-stop work, I think you owe yourself a holiday.' I replied that working with him and with Anna was as good as a holiday, but Herbert felt the London series had run its course. 'I need a bit of time to work out a new direction for you. This would be an ideal time for you to take a break. Have a change of scene. Spend all that dough you've been earning!'

My three years working with Herbert and Anna had brought great rewards, but the crowning moment was when the three of us received an invitation to meet Princess Elizabeth and Prince Philip at a private showing of *Spring*. After the film the Princess asked us about the technicalities of film-making, while Prince Philip talked cricket. As Anna and Herbert had both played for their schools and I still enjoy a bash at the wicket, there was plenty to talk about. They both expressed their enjoyment of the film. 'A real tonic,' remarked the Prince. 'Just what the public needs at the moment.' Members of the royal household also attended the viewing and the one criticism came from a figure wearing livery. 'If you'll forgive my saying so, Mr Wilding,' he said, 'you really don't spit on silver when you polish it, you use plate powder.'

The royal couple paid us the compliment of seeing *Spring* a second time when they attended a charity performance, at the end of which Anna and I came on stage and did our dream dance. I was recovering from a bad bout of pneumonia and the dance left me gasping. Afterwards, when we were presented, I was still feeling knocked out and must have looked it, for the Prince raised an eyebrow and said 'What's the matter with you? You look as if you've been having too many late nights!' 'But sir,' protested Anna, 'he has been very ill with pneumonia.' 'Then you shouldn't be here,' the Prince replied sternly.

Fame also brought money. I indulged in a picture-buying spree, mostly impressionists, telling myself that at least I was investing money as well as spending it. Then I lashed

out on what can only be called a *folie de grandeur*. I
bought myself a boat, with Stewart Granger. Since we
were both footloose bachelors with an eye for any pretty
women who came our way, we had much in common. But
the one thing I did not share with Stewart was his mania
for keeping fit. He used to arrive at my flat before
breakfast, drag me out of bed and try to talk me into gym
sessions before breakfast. When I told him they were not
my line, he was furious and snapped 'You eat my food,
you drink my wine, you fuck my women, yet you won't do
press-ups with me!'

Stewart also fancied himself as a sailor, although he did
not know the stern from the bow. Come to that, neither
did I. Our maiden voyage was a near-disaster. We set off
for France late at night. When our skipper retired to his
bunk, Stewart took over the wheel. But Stewart soon got
bored and called to me to take over while he went below.
Now I had never steered a boat before in my life and we
drifted round in circles before I got the hang of it. Then
suddenly through my night-glasses, which brought it
perilously close, I saw a huge liner sailing slap across our
bows. 'Oh boy,' I thought, 'I'm going to ram the liner!' I
called in alarm to Stewart, who hurried up on deck and
took a gander through the glasses. 'Crikey!' he said, and
then he issued his first and last naval command. 'Steer
round its ruddy arse!'

When we reached Le Touquet we tied up alongside
Errol Flynn's yacht, *The Medina*. During my brief stay in
Hollywood I had met Errol once or twice, but he greeted
me like a long-lost friend. 'Hiya, Mike,' he shouted,
waving from the deck. 'Bring your pal aboard for a drink.
I've got something I want you to see, an all-black
bathroom. It even has a black bidet!'

When I returned to work, Herbert had two surprises up his
sleeve. He had chosen a new screen-partner for my next
film, an up-and-coming French star, the adorable Odile
Versois. Herbert's other surprise left me flabbergasted. 'I

am promoting you to co-producer,' he told me calmly. 'But Herbert,' I protested, 'co-producers have to make decisions, don't they? I can't even decide whether to boil or poach my morning egg!'

But as usual, having made up his mind about something, Herbert stuck to his guns and I found myself seated behind a desk facing all the problems that go into the preparation of a film. So determined was I to make a success of my new-found role that I started off having a say in all departments, from the set/building to the artist's make-up, until Herbert dropped into my office and said quietly 'I appreciate the way you are wading into your new job, but if I may give you a word of advice, don't hire dogs and do all the barking yourself.'

In the new film, based on an idea by Nick Phipps, I played a stowaway on a boat belonging to a couple on a holiday cruise up the Seine. Odile played a girl cabin boy and the cast included those adroit players Jack Hulbert and Constance Cummings. What with our delightful location on the Seine itself and a bubbling script written mostly by Herbert, I hoped we had the makings of a successful lightweight comedy. But sadly it just did not come off. The picture's title was *Into the Blue*, but for ever afterwards Herbert wryly referred to it as 'Into the Red'. It was my first and last shot at producing. In future I stuck firmly to acting.

Paradoxically enough, it was I who unwittingly inspired the idea for our next film. Herbert, who had caught the picture-collecting bug from me, asked my advice about starting his own collection. Not feeling adequately equipped for such a task, I bought him some art books. About a week later he phoned and asked me to come round to his flat right away. 'Thanks to you,' he exclaimed, 'I think I've hit on an ideal subject for our next film!'

He showed me a colour reproduction of Frith's famous painting *Derby Day* in the book on British painting I had bought for him. 'I ask you,' he said, 'what more exciting film subject could we find? The Derby is a unique British institution, chiefly because its appeal is classless. The Cockney gets just as much of a kick out of his bob each way and a bag of winkles as an earl in his private box with his caviar and champagne.' *Derby Day* turned out to be something of an also-ran with the critics, but at least it was a winner at the box-office.

I thought Herbert was asking too much of me, though, when he told me of his next ploy, which was to co-star me with Anna in a film about Florence Nightingale. I was to play her benefactor and supporter, the statesman Sidney Herbert. 'But Herbert,' I protested, 'that's a serious character role. I'm not sure I'm up to it.' Herbert replied 'My guess is that you are a born character actor and here is a chance to prove it. And, by the way, you get off to a head start by being the great man's double.' To prove his point, before we started production, Herbert gave me a miniature of the great man and indeed the likeness was uncanny. I was also helped by Anna, who, as usual when she was portraying a historical character, buried herself in the history books of the era and gave me many tips.

The Lady with a Lamp brought about yet another meeting with the royal family, this time at a country house-party. Herbert had a new recruit in his team, the young and talented Lord John Brabourne, who joined us as a trainee producer. John was married to Lord Mountbatten's daughter Patricia and it so happened that Florence Nightingale herself had visited the family home, Broadlands, which made Anna long to see it. The upshot was that Lady Mountbatten invited Anna, Herbert and myself to a ball at Broadlands where the guests of honour were Princess Elizabeth and Prince Philip.

About midnight Brabourne said to me 'It's your turn next, Mike.' 'My turn for what?' I asked innocently. 'To dance with Her Royal Highness, of course.' I was absolutely aghast at the idea. 'I've had too much champagne!' I protested. 'I will tread on the royal toes!' Brabourne summoned a waiter and ordered black coffee.

Half an hour later I found myself being led reluctantly to the royal table. Brabourne introduced me to the Princess and when I asked her if she would like to dance, she smiled and said 'Indeed. But having seen you dance on the screen, I'm wondering whether I shall be up to it!' Then, with a nod of the head, she led the way to the dance floor. There were two bands present, playing alternately. One was a calypso group, who now rose to their feet and to my surprise and relief struck up a waltz. I blurted out 'Thank goodness! I was frightened they were going to play a rumba.' The Princess laughed. 'So was I,' she said. 'I can never get the hang of those Latin rhythms.'

After escorting her back to her table, I bowed and said 'I'm relieved I got through the dance without hitting you!' The Princess looked startled. What I had intended to say was 'without kicking you,' but 'kicking' sounded even worse and I was much too abashed to explain what I meant.

My next assignment brought two surprises. Herbert had the idea of casting me in the role of a detective in E. C. Bentley's famous mystery story *Trent's Last Case*. He also had a new leading lady who had come to fame in the 1940s, in particular with *Wicked Lady*. But in the 1950s Margaret Lockwood's name had unaccountably dropped out of the limelight. Herbert felt that the public would welcome a come-back and, judging by the subsequent reviews, how right he proved to be. Working with her was an education. She was such an out and out 'pro' – no retakes for Maggie, no hint of temperament. She turned out to be a most down-to-earth lady with a delicious sense of irony, mostly directed at herself.

It was also through *Trent* that I met Orson Welles. Two weeks into shooting Herbert had still not settled on the ideal actor to play the 'heavy'. 'Although his appearance in the film is brief,' Herbert explained to me, 'he must have a personality that will haunt the whole picture.'

One day, while discussing possible names, Herbert

casually said 'What about Orson Welles?' Maggie retorted 'What about God?' But once Herbert got an idea into his head there was no stopping him. 'Find Orson Welles,' he instructed his secretary. 'He could be in Rome or Paris or the wilds of Tibet, but find him!' After a global hunt Welles was finally tracked down in Hammersmith, in a cubby-hole of a cutting-room where he had hidden himself away editing *Macbeth*.

'Why all this secrecy?' Herbert asked. 'I'm lousy with writs,' Welles replied. 'If they catch up with me I'll never be able to finish my film.' Such news was manna from heaven to Herbert and he explained that although the role would only occupy ten minutes' screen time it was tailor-made for Welles's personality.

'Might do it,' Welles grunted, 'but I'm very busy and very expensive.' 'What's expensive?' 'For ten days' shooting, five thousand pounds.' Wilcox shook his head. 'No good, Orson, I could not contemplate such a sum.' 'What's your offer then?' asked Welles seeing the chance slipping away. 'Ten thousand.' replied Wilcox. Welles choked on his cigar. 'But that's twice my asking price!' 'I heard you,' replied Wilcox, 'but I've already earmarked ten thousand in my budget. That's what you're worth and that's what you're getting.'

On the set Welles kept the whole crew in a continual state of hysterics. Even Herbert became the butt of his asides. Herbert had the habit of extracting himself from a difficult moment in a scene by saying 'Never mind, we can always cut to this, that or the other.' Now Welles's scenes were, as they so often are in film-making, shot out of sequence. It happened that on the last day of filming they were shooting the opening scene. To enhance the drama of Welles's first appearance, Herbert had set up the shot so that his face was not seen by the audience, only the back of his head, as he sat in a chair puffing away at a cigar.

The first take did not satisfy Herbert, because the smoke from the cigar drifted away from the camera. So he stationed a props man to wave a board and make the smoke swirl in the desired direction. 'That's no good either,' said Herbert, exasperatedly, 'now the smoke is swirling too rapidly for reality.' Orson poked his head out from the back of the chair and, raising a sardonic eyebrow, said in his most soothing tone 'Never mind, Herbert, you can always cut to a dog wagging its tail.'

Trent's Last Case was a huge success, but the word 'last' proved all too prophetic, for it was the last film I ever made for Herbert. Only a few weeks earlier I would have dismissed such a possibility as absurd. Apart from our mutual affection we had nothing to gain and everything to lose by parting. Indeed, not long before, acting on the spur of the moment, I had dropped in to see Herbert at his Mount Street office. 'Well, is there anything particular on your mind?' he inquired. There was indeed. In fact, I had been thinking about it for some time. 'Yes, Herbert,' I replied, 'I want to talk to you about my contract.' 'I never talk to artists about money,' he said. 'Tell your agent to ring me.' 'What I have to say has nothing to do with money,' I countered. 'My contract with you is for ten years, isn't it?' Herbert nodded. 'Well,' I said, taking a deep breath, 'How would you feel about taking a chance and making it for twenty years?'

The very next day, in front of a battery of press and TV cameras, we signed what was surely a unique agreement. 'Nobody could have foreseen,' Herbert wrote, 'that within six months of signing that contract, all my future plans for Michael would be nullified by the whim and passions of a mere eighteen-year-old girl.'

The name of that mere eighteen-year-old girl was Elizabeth Taylor.

9
Liz

ELIZABETH Taylor has been one of the most maligned women of the twentieth century. She has been subjected to merciless attacks from columnists and gossip-writers, but they rarely mention the generosity of spirit which her friends know so well. Once a friend of Liz's, you are a friend for life – and if you are in trouble, Liz will be at your side before you have time to put down the telephone. Liz also has a strong maternal streak. She adores children and animals and is never happier than when surrounded by both. Above all she has in abundance a quality that I greatly admire, namely courage. She is undismayed by disaster, is afraid of no one and, when bullied by Hollywood tycoons, would often go on suspension rather than play an unsuitable role.

To begin at the beginning, when Liz arrived in England in 1951 to a hysterical crowd at London airport and a blaze of publicity, everybody in the business was clamouring to meet her. But to my mind she was still a child star and probably we would never have met at all had we not been working at the same studio. She was co-starring with Robert Taylor in *Ivanhoe* and I was just finishing *Trent's Last Case*.

Before we met I was already aware of her beauty. At lunch time in the canteen, instead of asking the waitress for the salt, she used to sashay down the whole length of the canteen to pick it up from the counter. Once during

one of these eye-boggling sashays Orson Welles, who was
lunching with me, raised a satirical eyebrow and said
'That girl didn't ought to do that, you know. Upsets the
digestion.' But so far as I was concerned she could do it as
often as she liked. I had never seen a more shattering
sashay.

Then one day we met in the studio corridor. It seemed
only natural that we should pass the time of day and
discuss our respective roles. But that's all there was to it, or
so I thought at the time. I had not reckoned on Liz's
determination. There were soon daily visits to the set. It
soon became clear, to my amazement, that she found a very
shy, middle-aged actor attractive.

By this time I was totally dazzled by her looks and
charm, but I didn't make a direct approach. Eventually,
she said to me plaintively 'I wish you'd stop treating me as
if I had a child's mind inside a woman's body.' Then blow
me down if she didn't come right out with it: 'Why don't
you invite me out to dinner tonight? You might change
your mind.'

I think I knew from our very first evening together that I
was completely hooked. But it was an emotion I fought for
several reasons. First, the age gap between us seemed
insuperable; secondly, I dreaded hurting Marlene. But I
was not very good at hiding my feelings from others. Anna
first saw us together at the Royal Film Performance of
Lady with a Lamp and wrote 'Michael could hardly keep
his eyes away from her and I noticed with amusement that
the attraction was mutual.' Mutual attraction by now it
certainly was. The press began to hound us wherever we
went and the gossip-columns were full of speculation
about our romance. In fact, I was in a terrible dilemma,
which Herbert succinctly put in a nutshell: 'One night,
Michael arrived at our flat looking particularly worried.
He then confided in me that he thought he was in love
with two very different women at the same time. "Which
one shall I marry, Herbert?" he asked, "Liz or Marlene?"
"If you marry Marlene," I told him, "everyone will say

you are marrying your grandmother. If you marry Liz you will be accused of cradle-snatching.'"'

Herbert recalls that when my engagement to Liz was announced he happened to be lunching with Marlene in New York. 'She was very sad,' he wrote. ' "What's Liz Taylor got that I haven't got?" I didn't have the heart to give her the obvious answer, namely youth.'

But it was Liz's extreme youth that held me back from declaring my affection. The age gap had become a sort of bugbear between us, frightening me and infuriating Liz. I remember arriving one night at her hotel to take her out to dinner. Unpunctuality is a sort of disease with Liz and as usual she wasn't ready, so she called me into the bedroom where she was making up her face. I said 'I can't think why anyone as beautiful as you puts on so much make-up.' 'It's to make me look older,' she replied and suddenly her eyes filled with tears. 'If only I was older, you would ask me to marry you.' 'Twenty years is a big gap,' I told her gently; 'I wouldn't want you to find out you'd made a mistake.' Through her tears, Liz lashed out angrily 'Tomorrow I'm flying to California. When I'm gone you'll see who's making the mistake!'

How right she was. When I saw her off at the airport next day I felt like crying myself. But Liz wasn't crying. She was furious. 'Goodbye, Mr Shilly-shally,' she blazed, 'Let's forget we ever met!' I went through a week of misery, then sent her a cable: *Am catching the next plane to Hollywood, signed Mr Shilly-shally.*

She was at Burbank airport to meet me. Oblivious of the barrage of press photographers, we hugged and kissed and laughed and cried at the sheer joy of our reunion. Also there to meet me was Stewart Granger with his new wife, Jean Simmons, who was just twenty-two. We became the talk of the town as a regular foursome, going everywhere together. Stewart said to me 'I can't think what these youngsters see in us oldsters, can you?' 'That question is baffling me out of my forty-year-old mind,' I replied. To which Stewart retorted 'To hear you carry on, anyone would think you were going through a male menopause. Forget you're forty. I have, and look how happy I am.'

But, despite Stewart's example, it was Liz who finally popped the question. We were having dinner at Romanoff's when I produced a sapphire and diamond ring I had bought for her earlier that day. I reached for her right hand but she snatched it away, putting out her left hand and waggling her third finger. 'That's where it belongs,' she said. Then admiring the ring, which now adorned the third finger of her left hand, she kissed me and said 'That makes it official doesn't it? Or shall I spell it out for you? Dear Mr Shilly-shally, will you marry me?'

Liz was all for making the announcement the next day, but we decided to wait until I could break the news to Herbert. I felt I owed him that courtesy at least, although with the announcement of Liz's divorce from Nick Hilton and the papers' speculation about a runaway marriage in Las Vegas Herbert must have known what was about to happen.

Leaving Liz to follow a week later, I flew back to England and as soon as I arrived rang Herbert and invited myself round to his flat. Although the bubbly flowed as ever, I was aware that Herbert was not his usual effervescent self. At last he said 'You have the air of a man with something on his mind. Let's have it.'

I blurted out 'I have asked Liz to marry me. Or rather it was the other way round. But it amounts to the same thing.' Herbert played dumb. 'What's the matter,' he joshed, 'has she turned you down?' 'No, amazingly she likes the idea.' 'Then why the long face?' 'Because it means I will have to go and live with her in Hollywood.' Herbert reflected and then asked quietly 'What's to become of our twenty-year contract?' 'That's just it,' I replied. 'That's what's making me so miserable. I've come to ask you to release me from it.'

It was Anna who rose to the occasion and came to my rescue. 'I'm sure', she said, 'that neither Herbert nor I would wish to stand in the way of your happiness.'

Herbert nodded. 'I'd be the last man in the world to want an unhappy actor on my hands. Here's wishing happiness to you both. But if you'll forgive me saying so, I don't think Hollywood will understand you, or vice versa. I've said it before and I'm saying it again.'

What prophetic words! But at a press conference next day, when asked his reaction to our break-up, all Herbert said was 'Let's say Mike had a better offer, a lifer!'

The engagement was officially announced on 14 February 1952. A week later Liz flew in from Hollywood. I have seen some wild displays of public hysteria, but none to equal the circus that greeted her arrival. As we made our way through the mob of fans to the VIP lounge, Liz's dress was literally torn from her shoulders and some even tried to pull out locks of her hair. Liz is a tough little dab and accustomed to fans' frenzy, but on that day I could see she was really frightened. Once she was safely in the VIP lounge her first words were 'Gee, I'm glad to be alive!' and when asked if it was she who had done the proposing she answered gaily 'It's leap year, so I leapt!' About her future career she said 'A career isn't all that important really. When I'm married to Mike, I don't even care if I stop acting.' And, when questioned about our plans for a family, she replied happily 'Of course we want three or four children – or as long as it takes me to produce a son!'

Two hectic weeks later our wedding took place, on 27 February 1952. The *Daily Mirror* claimed that it created even more of a stir than the Windsor marriage. Thanks to my nerves and Liz's unpunctuality it was nearly the marriage that never was. In her autobiography Anna vividly describes the scene at the Berkeley, where Liz was getting ready for the ceremony:

'I had suggested that I was sure "Churchie" our wardrobe supervisor would love to help Liz dress. As arranged I arrived at the Berkeley Hotel, where she was to stay overnight, one hour before we were due to leave for Caxton Hall. The hall porter 'phoned the room – line engaged. He then called the chambermaid who said the

"do not disturb" sign was still outside Miss Taylor's door.
In desperation I explained that I must go up. I knocked on
the door - no answer. A second knock and as it opened, I
saw Churchie's anguished face - in her hand a bunch of
keys. "Miss Taylor's still in bed," she said, "and there are
six trunks and I don't know where to look for the wedding
dress. What am I to do?" She was nearly in tears. I went
into the bedroom, Liz was on the telephone. "I'll never
make it, Mike," she was saying. She waved gaily to me,
smiled that devastating smile and went on talking. I
looked at the stack of luggage. I understood Churchie's
dilemma. "Where's the dress?" I mouthed to Liz. She
pointed to two trunks. There it was in the first Churchie
opened - an exquisite pearl-grey dress designed for her by
the head designer of MGM Studios. Forty minutes later,
with a radiant Liz, I left the hotel.'

Meanwhile, back at my flat Herbert arrived ready to take
up his duties as best man. He took one look at me and said
'What you need is a bumper brandy. Really, Mike, I've
heard of bridegroom's nerves, but you're a hospital
case!' During the drive to Caxton Hall Herbert tried to
calm me down as I said over and over again 'Am I doing
the right thing, Herbert? Am I doing the right thing?' By
some miracle, due mostly to Anna and Churchie, Liz was
only twenty minutes late. Another ten minutes and I swear
I would not have been there to marry her.

The ceremony over, extra police arrived to make a way
for us through the wildly cheering crowd. When we drove
off, there were fans actually standing on the running-
boards and they clung on until we pulled up at Claridges,
which was besieged by another hysterical mob. The
reception was constantly interrupted by fans below in the
street yelling 'Liz! Mike! Let's see you!' Liz was all for
appearing on the balcony, but I demurred. 'We are not
royalty,' I said, 'and not circus performers.' 'Don't be so
pompous,' said Liz, 'they only want to share our
happiness.' So we went out on the balcony, but the fans
continued chanting until we made our exit to the waiting

car amid such a scramble that even the dignified commissionaire lost his hat. Liz tossed her bouquet into the crowd, who fell on it and tore it to bits. My last memory of the day was a remark from one of MGM's press agents. 'To think this was supposed to be a quiet wedding!'

10
Hollywood Spree

WE started our married life in Hollywood facing a heavily mortgaged future. True, MGM had just signed up Liz for a new seven-year contract and at the same time, chiefly I'm sure to keep Liz happy, they signed me up for three years. Yet within weeks of signing we both found ourselves consigned to limbo when MGM put us both under suspension and cancelled our salaries until further notice.

Liz had just finished *The Girl Who Had Everything*, an apt title, seeing that she was now pregnant. I was classified as a rebel when I refused a role in *Latin Lovers*, from which Lana Turner and Fernando Lamas had backed out, since I was determined not to start my Hollywood career by making a rubbishy film and Liz was equally adamant that she would not appear in roles that did not suit her. The upshot was that MGM instantly added our names to the black list and, partly because of her pregnancies, between us Liz and I ran up record suspension time for any married couple in the entire history of motion pictures.

Despite our suspension, with heads in the clouds we started house-hunting. We soon found that the kind of house we were looking for cost $60,000 to $80,000, but Liz was undeterred. 'Let's find the house, then we'll worry about the money,' she said. Well, at last we did find the house. Driving up in Laurel Canyon one day, Liz spotted a 'For Sale' notice on the gates of a driveway leading up to a rambling white house built on a mountainside. That same afternoon when we looked it over with the agent I fell in love with it too. The house had vast windows in every room with a view of the Pacific on one side and mountains on the other. The grounds were ablaze with crimson sequoia trees and the centrepiece was a giant swimming-pool. It was the ideal house for an outdoor person like Liz. But when the agent told me that the asking price was $150,000 my enthusiasm cooled. 'It's no good,' I protested. 'In our circumstances such a sum is impossible.' 'Anything is possible if you want it badly enough,' retorted Liz. 'We'll raise the money somehow.'

Next day she drew out $47,000 worth of bonds saved since her childhood. Naturally, I contributed my own savings, but that still left us about $10,000 short. 'There's only one thing for it,' declared Liz, 'I shall have to ask MGM for an advance on my salary.'

She was as good as her word. When she returned from MGM she said in a flat little voice 'Well, I got the ten grand.' Then she burst into tears. 'The absolute sods!' she raged. 'They made me feel it was a crime to be having a baby instead of making a film. I as good as went down on my knees to beg for a lousy ten grand. I swear I'll never ask for a penny ever again!'

Within a month we were installed in our dream house, both of us in a state of idiotic happiness. Liz quickly filled the house with a variety of animals, including two poodles, three cats and a tame duck, which perched on her shoulder. As each day passed she became more ecstatically happy about being pregnant, even though she was not having an easy time. She had frequent dizzy spells and was sick every morning. But she laughed it off. 'Every time I am sick,' she would say, 'I feel more like a mother!'

When the great day finally arrived, her doctors decided she needed to have a Caesarean section. She waved to me gaily as they wheeled her off to the operating-theatre. Anyone would have thought she was off to a tea party.

36 Our names in lights, in Leicester Square

37 Marlene and me out on the town

38 *The Law and the Lady* – stepping out with Greer Garson and
Fernando Lamas during a break in shooting

39 Partners in crime – with Greer Garson in *The Law and the Lady*

Michael Howard Wilding, a fine, bouncing eight pounds, was delivered safely on 6 January 1953. But Liz suffered more than her share of post natal discomfort, with a great deal of pain, and had to remain in hospital for three weeks.

The following year she gave birth to our second son, Christopher. A week before his expected arrival Liz said to me 'I'm going to have this one for my birthday.' When I suggested she enjoy her birthday and have the Caesarean the following week, she shook her head and said joyfully 'What better birthday present could I have than a baby?'

During those two years Liz had, of course, been on studio suspension. A friend remarked to her at the time that having two children had cost her a million dollars. 'I wouldn't care if they'd cost two million,' Liz retorted. 'They're worth it.'

Those first two years of our marriage were among the best years of my life. We were both deeply in love and deliriously happy, regardless of the fact that we were living in a kind of cloud-cuckoo-land, always existing on borrowed money. The truth is that Liz and I shared the same careless outlook on life, living as if there were no tomorrow. We were both lazy and basically unambitious, needing money, but spending it like drunken sailors. We got a great deal of pleasure from giving each other expensive presents which we could not afford. Life, we both thought, was all too short, so why not enjoy it?

Yet during those first few years of our marriage neither of us courted Hollywood social life. We were happy enough lazing by the pool playing poker, which was the current Hollywood craze, and we were so involved with each other and our children that we did not seek outside company. The one exception was the British set, who went out of their way to make us feel welcome. Our first invitation came from my old chum from Ealing Studio days, C. Aubrey Smith. Now over eighty, he had retired and was famous both for organising cricket matches and for giving tea parties. As we drove up his driveway I spotted an odd-looking object standing on the roof of his house. Reaching the front door, I looked up to get a better view. To my amusement, I saw it was a weather vane consisting of three cricket stumps with bails on top.

One famous, or perhaps infamous, member of the British set, whom I was delighted to meet again, was Errol Flynn. Within a week of our arrival in Hollywood he invited me to visit his new home. 'Mortgaged up to the hilt, old man,' he said gaily, 'but it has one great advantage.'

Flynn's house was at the top of Mulholland Drive, a very swish residential area which ran along the crest of the hills overlooking San Fernando Valley. He met me at the doorway with a bottle in his hand and after we had had a couple of drinks, led me out into the garden and pointed to the lights of Hollywood twinkling below us. 'You know why I chose this house?' he asked. 'Well, let me tell you. Standing here I can piss down on Warner Brothers' studios!'

'Now,' he said, 'come and have a look at my private den.' This turned out to be a dimly lit room with walls covered with photographs of naked ladies. 'All taken by myself,' announced Errol proudly. After I had shown due interest, for I always have eyes for the feminine form, particularly when unadorned, he led me back to the drawing-room, where to my surprise I saw standing in pride of place on the mantelshelf a large picture of John Barrymore. Looking at it closer, I saw that it was inscribed with the odd salutation 'From one drunken sot to another. Affectionately, John Barrymore.' Full of curiosity, I asked Flynn how he had got to know the great actor and he told me the following story.

Unknown to either his friends or his fans, Flynn in his youth, under the tutelage of his father who was a professor at Trinity College Dublin, was a brilliant scholar, excelling in Latin, history and literature. Although appalled by his son's decision to become an actor, his father had nevertheless paid for him to go to Hollywood.

With high hopes, Flynn had boarded the Super Chief, the luxury train which used to run from New York to Hollywood. 'Even in those days,' recalled Errol, 'I'd developed a taste for John Barleycorn, so I made straight for the bar and who should I find myself sitting next to but the great man himself. After about the second drink, I had enough nerve to introduce myself by telling him that my mother's greatest theatrical memory was of seeing his *Hamlet* in London in 1926.'

Barrymore was evidently quite taken aback and exclaimed 'Fancy anyone remembering that I was once not a bad actor. Of course, *Hamlet* came easy to me. Can never make up my own mind about anything except when it's time to order the next drink. What is your tipple, dear boy?' 'We spent the next hour drinking neat bourbons,' recalled Errol, 'while Barrymore warned me of the perils of Hollywood. He called it "an actors' cemetery".'

My most lasting memory of Flynn is of an incident which proved he was a true sportsman. He had invited Liz and me to be his guests in his private box at Santa Anita racecourse. Liz was working, but I jumped at the chance to get away from lounging about the house. When he came to pick me up, he had as his companions the current Miss Sweden and Miss Norway. Flynn frequently shared his favours quite openly between two or three women at one time, and they seemed quite happy to go along with such an arrangement.

When we reached the box, Errol turned to me and said 'Look old chum, I'm being chased by at least a couple of bums waiting to serve writs on me for alimony to at least two wives. I'm safe here in my private box, but I don't want to venture outside in case they spot me. Will you be a sport and place my bets for me?' Taking a wad of hundred-dollar bills from his pocket, he peeled off a couple and handed them to me with the name of the horse of his choice. Well, Errol may have been lucky with the ladies, but his luck certainly did not include the gee-gees. For every race he peeled off another couple of hundred bucks and either his fancy never got out of the starting-gate or it finished last.

In the last race two horses were running which had similar names, something like Ice Maiden and Frozen Lady. As before, I went down to the tote betting office and placed Errol's last two hundred greenbacks on the horse of his choice, Frozen Lady. At least, I thought it was the horse of his choice. But, as the runners came up the straight towards the winning post, I was amazed to see Errol jumping to his feet and shouting jubilantly 'Come on Ice Maiden! You dolly! You darling! You've saved my bacon!'

'My God,' I thought, 'I've backed the wrong horse!' With Ice Maiden winning by two lengths at odds of twenty-to-one, Errol should have recouped his losses and have gone home with a notecase full of hundred-dollar bills, so I had to own up. The two dollies confirmed that Errol had distinctly picked Ice Maiden.

'How much would you have won, Errol?' I asked. 'Let me make you out a cheque.' 'Keep your cheque-book in your pocket,' said Errol. 'It's my own fault for using you as a donkey boy.' When I protested that I would like to make good my mistake, he said 'All of us make mistakes, but that doesn't mean we have to pay for them. I make a point of never paying for mine.' Then he put an arm round my shoulders and said 'Not to worry, dear boy. All the lolly would have gone to my ex-wives anyway!'

The last time I saw him it was evident that, with an average intake of a bottle of vodka a day, he was pursuing a suicidal path. 'Errol,' I asked, 'it's none of my business, so you can tell me to go to hell, but why do you drink so much? You are killing yourself, you must know that.' In reply, he downed his vodka and said 'Inside this Hollywood playboy is a someway decent actor waiting for a chance to prove it. But, since Hollywood will never give me that chance, I drink to obliviate that decent actor. When I'm sober his cries are too loud for comfort, so I stay drunk to deafen his claims. Is that too difficult to understand?'

Yet on seeing the last picture he made before he died, *Roots of Heaven*, in which he played a drunken ex-doctor, everyone in Hollywood saluted a great performance. But when I rang to congratulate him, he said bitterly that along with the praise had come the innuendo that he was only playing himself. 'In point of fact, I didn't drink a drop during the whole production. You see, here was my first real acting opportunity and I knew the one thing you cannot do is to portray a drunk when you are anything but sober.'

Besides the British set there was also the Hollywood set, including Robert Taylor, with whom Liz had starred in *Ivanhoe*, and his new wife, Ursula Thiess , who became regular visitors. Bob once told me 'You know, Mike, I proposed to Liz before you did. It wasn't exactly what you would call a conventional proposal. I said to Liz "We both have the same colouring – blue eyes and black hair. We could have fabulous-looking kids and we could sell them." I meant it as a joke, of course, but she took me seriously and was more than a bit shocked. "Sell them for what?" she asked. "For enormous profit," I replied.'

Like everyone else I was greatly saddened by Robert Taylor's premature death. He was such a decent all-rounder, always telling stories against himself. There was one he used to tell about when he was living at the top of Topanga Canyon, where bush fires were a frequent occurrence. One night, just after they had moved in, a fire spread to the grounds of their mansion. 'In great panic,' Taylor told me, 'I phoned the fire brigade, then I took all the valuable pictures off the walls, scooped up my wife's jewellery and piled them into our station-wagon and drove with all speed down the now flaming driveway. We had gone about fifty yards when I suddenly stopped and reversed. "The kids!" I yelled to my wife. "We've forgotten the kids!"'

When I arrived in Hollywood I had four idols whom I

dearly wished to meet. Naturally, I hadn't the nerve to approach any of them, but I was lucky enough to meet three of them by accident. The first I met on my very first day at MGM. A publicity representative was giving me a guided tour of the studios. I felt overawed by the vastness of the place. Thirty-two sound stages! Three back lots large enough to contain permanently built sets of anything from an English village to an old-time Western town. We had nothing like it in England. It was like being shown round the suburbs of a vast city.

At last I was led onto a sound stage where a dance rehearsal was in progress. My heart leapt. It was Gene Kelly up there dancing. What a perfectionist! He would rehearse the same step over and over again until he was satisfied. Came the break and a sweating, breathless Kelly jumped down from the stage. He took one look at me and vigorously pumped my hand. 'Welcome to Uncle Sam's prison, Mr Wilding,' he said. 'Happy to meet a new slave!' I was amazed that he should know my name and flattered when he told me he had made a special trek to the local art cinema where he had seen *Spring in Park Lane*.

'Not bad,' he said, 'not bad at all. Your comedy is fine. But as for your dancing . . .' He wagged a forefinger under my nose disapprovingly. 'You're not supposed to dance at all, you know? I'm allowed to dance, so is Fred Astaire. But I wouldn't try it if I were you!'

The meeting with my second idol was much more of a coincidence. We both happened to be lunching at the Brown Derby, but the reason for our encounter goes back to the filming of *Under Capricorn*. There was a scene where I had to walk on a treadmill while in back projection the scenery of Sydney flashed by. I had just completed this boring exercise for the third time when the assistant director asked for yet another take. Half jokingly and half in anger, I retorted 'If you know how to do it so well, why don't you fucking well do it yourself?'

Well, in Hollywood, where actors are supposed to

behave like sheep, rumour soon spread that here was one who had dared to answer back, even if it was only to an assistant director. Like all stories in Hollywood it had swiftly passed into the actors' book of legends.

'Your name's Wilding, isn't it?' inquired Spencer Tracy gruffly when he saw me. I nodded apprehensively. 'Are you the son of a gun who actually told a director to "fucking well do it himself"?' demanded Tracy. Again I nodded. He slapped me on the back. 'Well done, you limey son of a bitch!' he beamed. 'I've been wanting to do the same thing for years, but never had the guts!'

This was the first of many meetings. We both had the same approach to our profession. I remember him saying to me one day 'You know I never know how to reply when people ask me about the secret of acting. You see I don't act. I just am the person I am playing. Does that make sense?'

It made perfect sense to me, for I tackled the job the same way. He was a great character, warm yet introverted when it came to talking about himself, but he had a whimsical sense of humour when assessing his fellow artists and our boss, the great Sam Goldwyn. Goldwyn's unwitting misuses of the English language, such as 'A verbal contract is not worth the paper it's written on', have passed into legend. Neither as a new employee nor during the whole course of my contract was I granted an interview. Yet within two weeks of my arrival in Hollywood I could boast that I had heard two Goldwynisms for the price of one.

I was attending a luncheon party given in honour of Field-Marshal Mongomery. The climax to the star-studded occasion was when Goldwyn rose to make a speech. 'It is my great pleasure and honour', he announced, 'to introduce to you all our guest of honour, Marshall Field von Montgomery.' The fact that Marshall Field is one of America's biggest department stores made it a double gaffe!

The encounter with my third Hollywood idol happened one afternoon while Liz was at the studio. I was painting when the doorbell rang. My hands covered in paint, I opened the door to find myself face to face with Marilyn Monroe, some clothes draped over her arm. In that unforgettably husky little-girl voice she said 'Would you think it dreadful of me as a perfect stranger to ask you a favour?' I recovered myself sufficiently to reply 'Ask away.'

Shyly, she explained that her studio had suggested the exterior of my house as being a picturesque background for some publicity stills. Then, pointing at the clothes draped over her arm, she blurted out 'You see, I need some place to change my costumes.' 'Say no more,' I said, 'Welcome to Chez Wilding.' With a mock bow I ushered her into the hall, explaining that, as my wife was out, she was welcome to use her bedroom. 'Thank you so very much,' she murmured. Then, with a sudden dimpling smile, she added impishly 'It's odd isn't it? I'm more used to taking off my clothes than putting them on.'

Half an hour later there was a timid knock and Marilyn, peering through the half-open study door, said 'I just kinda wanted to thank you for your hospitality.' I jumped to my feet and said 'Come on in.' She swayed towards me and I noticed beads of perspiration trickling down her forehead. Sitting her on the couch, I said 'You look as if you could do with a drink. How about a glass of champagne?' Leaning back wearily, she lisped 'Bliss. Sheer bliss.'

When I returned a few minutes later with a bottle and a couple of glasses, she greeted me with a wan smile and asked 'Do you mind if I take my shoes off? I always take my shoes off when I'm feeling kind of all in.' 'Take off anything you like,' I replied, adding quickly 'I meant that only in the nicest way.' She gave me that rainbow smile again and murmured 'You Englishmen only ever mean anything in the nicest way.' Suddenly she caught sight of her reflection in a mirror on the wall and with a grimace asked plaintively 'Do I look as lousy as I feel?' Before I could reply she said angrily 'It's all right. You can come out with the truth which is more than mirrors ever do! If you follow me?' 'Not exactly,' I confessed. She cupped her face in her hands and, speaking with the intensity of a child trying to make an impression, she burst out 'Haven't you ever known the feeling that inside you were falling to bits, like a cracked egg? I often feel that way and then I look in the mirror and expect to see my face all coming apart. You know, your eyes pointing in the wrong directions and you have two noses? You know what I mean, a face like a Picasso painting? Just by looking at it you know he's painting a person who's crying inside. My doctor tells me that crying is good for one. But, you see, I can't cry. No matter how bad I feel, I can't cry.'

'Your doctor's right,' I replied gently. 'Tears are a way of letting off steam.' She drained her glass and announced that she was due back at the studios in half an hour. At the front door, she put her hand in mine. 'I'll remember what you said today about crying being good for you. Maybe, if I try hard enough, I'll learn the knack.'

I fear she never did learn to cry except on the screen. Perhaps that is why she died so tragically young – not by intent, I am sure, but perhaps having sought in sleep a release that she was not able to find in tears.

No incident was to bring me more lasting happiness than my encounter with my fourth, and greatest, Hollywood idol. For once, such was my eagerness to meet her, I took the initiative. During my first visit to Hollywood I heard she was staying in my hotel. To gain courage I ordered a drink, which took half an hour to arrive, but still I could not lift the receiver. So I ordered another drink. That took another half-hour and I remember saying to myself 'It's now or never', then picking up the telephone and asking for her room. A voice said 'Hello' – a low, vibrant, throbbing voice. There was no mistaking it. 'Miss Garland?' I heard myself saying. 'I admire your work so much and as you are staying at the same hotel I just had to call you.' 'What did you say your name was?' the vibrant voice inquired. 'Wilding,' I repeated. There was a gurgle of pleasure at the end of the phone. 'Not Michael Wilding?' she asked. 'Are you as witty as in your films?' 'Alas no,' I replied. 'After one drink you'd soon find out I'm as dull as ditch water.' Once again that delicious little gurgle of a laugh came down the phone. 'You certainly have a back-handed way of asking a girl out for a drink. I'll meet you in the lounge in five minutes.'

She was wearing green and, as she came into the lounge, she reminded me of an elf. But there was nothing elfin about the blaze in those glorious brown eyes. We seemed to be on the same wavelength at once and we laughed a lot, so that two hours went by in a flash. Then she looked at her watch in horror. 'I was due at the studio ages ago,' she said. 'But first I must take my uppers.' She opened her handbag, took out a small medicine bottle, poured half a dozen blue pills into the palm of her hand, popped them in her mouth and swilled them down with the remainder of her drink. 'But Judy,' I protested, 'do you know those are purple hearts?' She nodded. 'I call them my "uppers". The yellow ones are my "downers".' Horrified, I asked her how long she had been taking drugs.

One day when Judy was sixteen and had done four films on the trot for MGM, she collapsed from exhaustion while rehearsing a dance number. 'The director called the studio doctor and told him I had to get through that number that day as the set was to be dismantled. "Don't worry," said the doctor, "here's something that will pull you through." The doctor produced a bottle of pills and I took some. He told me to go lie down in my dressing-room for ten minutes and I'd feel on top of the world. Sure enough, he was right. But I didn't sleep all that night and arrived at the studio the next day feeling like a wreck. Once again the doc gave me some of the blue pills, but he also gave me a bottle of yellow pills. "If you have any trouble sleeping," he said, "take a couple of these."' Judy wrinkled her nose at my horrified face. 'Lots of stars take them. But I hate them because from the age of sixteen I've been on a sort of treadmill. Living, working on my "uppers" and sleeping on my "downers". If you ask me, Hollywood turned me into a walking drugstore. What's more, I'm scared that as I get older I will have to take more and more of both of them to keep going. But one day, I swear, I'm going to take some time off the treadmill. I'm going to break the habit because I want more than anything in the world to stand on my own two feet. As it is, I'm living on crutches.'

I was deeply angered by the widespread suggestions that 'as a drug-addict, she brought about her own destruction'. It was Hollywood that first put her on the treadmill and Hollywood that was responsible for her early death.

Two other Hollywood incidents haunt me to this day. Each in its own way revealed to me the reality behind the outward glitter. The first concerns a person I shall always think of as 'The Lady of the Camellias', for she was wearing them in her hair the last time we met. Four years earlier, on my first visit to Hollywood, my impression of her in the Polo Lounge of the Beverly Hills Hotel was rather different. I thought she was a female bar-fly.

Perhaps because it was nearing midnight and there was a taxi strike, the Polo Lounge was almost deserted. I had just ordered a drink when I heard a tearful female voice coming from the other end of the bar. 'Please, Frankie, gimme just one more drink. A teeny one?' The barman replied 'No, Ma'am, I'm not serving you any more drinks tonight.' I turned to see a small blonde, probably in her late thirties, wrapped in mink, clinging to the bar for support. 'Please, Frankie,' she pleaded, near tears, 'just one until my taxi arrives.' 'Now lady,' replied the barman, gently but firmly, 'you know there are no taxis operating tonight.' The little blonde started to sob. 'How am I going to get home?' she wailed. 'That's your problem, lady,' replied the barman, 'you could go to the front desk and try ordering a car.' With a great effort, she got down from the bar-stool and began tottering to the door; she had only managed a few steps when she fell in a heap at my feet. Now, I'm not in the habit of playing knight in shining armour to lady drunks, but I found myself helping her to her feet and saying 'I have a car outside. Can I help by giving you a lift home?'

She nodded, unable to speak, and still sobbing clung to my arm as I half carried her to the car park. My car was a convertible and as soon as I had propped her up in the front seat, I pressed the button to lower the hood. She put her hands to her head and cried, 'My hair! It will blow all over the place. What will my husband think?' I remember thinking that in her condition the last thing her husband would worry about was her hair-style. But all I said was 'You need some fresh air. There is nothing like oxygen for clearing the head. Take big gulps of it.'

As we drove off, much to my relief, I saw that she was taking in great gasps of air. She had managed to give me an address up in the swish Bel Air district, which was about half an hour's drive away. But I deliberately drove slowly in the hope that she would begin to sober up. Sure enough, in about ten minutes she took out her compact and began cleaning up her mascara-stained cheeks and repairing her make-up. As I glanced at the reflection in her mirror it suddenly struck me that I had seen that face before, but for the life of me I could not put a name to it.

Out of the blue, in a steady voice, she suddenly said 'You're right about oxygen', then she covered her face with her hands and cried in a muffled voice 'Oh, how I hate myself for getting drunk.' 'Do you do it often?' I asked. She nodded her head. 'Yes, but only lately.' She did not speak again until we reached the floodlit gateway to an imposing house. 'Stop here,' she said. 'I'll tell my husband a friend gave me a lift.' Suddenly she reached out and touched my arm. 'Anyway, you are a friend. A friend in need.' She paused for a second, then she said, 'I expect you are wondering why I got drunk?' 'That's your business,' I replied, 'but I wouldn't make a habit of it.'

'That's just it,' she went on, 'you see it makes me forget.' 'Forget what?' I asked, not truly interested. Her reply sent a chill down my spine. 'I have cancer and I haven't long to live. But I haven't told anybody, not even my husband.' 'He should be the first to know,' I cried aghast, 'he could give you the comfort you need.' 'No,' she said dully, 'you see my husband is a very religious man. I used to have faith too. But now I've lost it and knowing that would break his heart.' I put my arm round her shoulders. 'Forgive me talking like a Dutch uncle,' I said, 'but he must know you've taken to the bottle?' She nodded. 'Well,' I said, 'that must be breaking his heart. Tell him the whole truth. If he is a truly religious man he will not only understand your losing faith, he will help you get it back.' 'Maybe you're right,' she said. 'Anyway, what have I to lose by giving it a try?' 'You have everything to gain,' I assured her. She nodded, then bent forward and kissed me on the forehead. The next moment she got out of the car. I stayed and watched her little figure walking steadily up the driveway until she was out of sight. We had not exchanged names and I certainly never expected to see her again.

Four years later I found out her identity. William Powell, a close friend of ours, gave a party to celebrate our wedding anniversary. It was around nine o'clock and the party was in full swing. I was about to ask Liz for the first dance, when I saw him come through the door – Bing Crosby. But my eyes nearly fell out of my head when I saw clinging lovingly to his arm my damsel in distress. But what a transformation! She was dressed in white satin and tulle and wore a garland of camellias in her blonde curls and was obviously glowing with happiness.

Powell pounced on the couple and led them straight to our table. 'Well,' beamed Bing, 'if it isn't the newly-weds. Happy anniversary to both of you.' Then he turned to the radiant creature at his side and said. 'Meet the wife, Dixie Lee Crosby.' As we shook hands I saw the flash of recognition in her eyes. I put my finger to my lips and winked. She got the message and said how do you do in the most formal manner. They sat down at our table and Bing said at once 'May I borrow your lovely wife for a whirl round the floor?' 'Providing I can have the honour of dancing with yours,' I said.

As soon as we hit the dance floor, Dixie's pent-up emotion produced a flood of gratitude. 'How wonderful we should meet again! Now at last I have a chance to thank you. You see I took your advice. I told Bing everything. About my illness, my loss of faith. He was wonderful. I know my days are numbered, but through Bing I have learned not to be afraid of death. If anything we are closer than we have ever been because every day is a sort of bonus. I never drink now. I feel a new woman. Do I look different?' 'You look like a Botticelli come to life,' I replied truthfully. 'We must tell Bing about how you helped me. He would wish to thank you.' I shook my head. 'Not a word,' I said, 'and that's an order. You took the decision. I only offered advice.' Only a few weeks later I learned that she had died peacefully in her sleep.

My most lasting memory of Hollywood is one of sheer tragedy. It was a shock to learn that so fine an actor as John Garfield was a banned name. It was the script-writer Ben Hecht, one of the few friends I made while with MGM, who first told me Garfield's story. After a brilliant film career spanning twenty years, during which time he won an Oscar for his supporting role in *Gentleman's Agreement*, Garfield had not made a film since 1950 after his courageous stand against McCarthy's Un-American Activities Committee. Unlike the 'Famous Ten', the writers who took the same brave stand and as a result were sentenced to a year's imprisonment, Garfield had not been sent to prison. But he suffered a punishment that in the long run was perhaps even worse. He was sent to Hollywood's equivalent of Coventry.

He was fired out of hand from his studio, Warner Brothers, who declared that the remainder of his twenty-year contract was null and void. Overnight his name appeared on the Hollywood black list and no studio would employ him. In desperation he turned to Broadway, where a decade earlier he had made his name in Clifford Odet's play *Golden Boy* and could have expected to be welcomed back with open arms. Instead, he discovered that the McCarthy hysteria had spread its net nation-wide. No producer would even agree to meet him, let alone offer him work. After two years in the wilderness he returned to Hollywood. But Jack Warner symbolised the film city's reception when he cut him dead publicly in the Brown Derby, and the rest of the community followed suit.

The ordeal took severe toll of his health as well as his finances and, finally, he ended up renting a tumbledown shack on the outskirts of Santa Monica where, according to Hecht, he lived like a hermit, aggravating a deteriorating heart condition by taking to the bottle.

One day I found myself wandering into a sleazy joint known as 'Barney's Beanery', a ramshackle barn of a place on the wrong side of Sunset Boulevard, notorious for the down-and-out character of its patrons. It was a haven for extras, out-of-work bit players, has-beens and have-nots, and was owned and run by an ex-prizefighter, an eccentric Irishman called Barney. But regulars addressed him as 'Prince Barney' as an ironic comment on a very different rendezvous where the self-styled 'Prince Romanoff' held sway over high society. The latter would allocate you a table according to your current star rating. 'Prince Barney' was just as choosy in his own way. If he didn't like your face, you were shown the door by one of Barney's musclemen.

What, you may ask, was I doing in such a place? Well, at that time Liz was working, but I very definitely was not. The only break in my lonely day was a lunch-time visit to Liz at the studio and soon enough being an out-of-work husband of a big star began to pall. There I was surrounded by famous names all in make-up doing a day's work, while I tagged along at Liz's side like a tame poodle.

In the end I opted out of these daily rituals and used to settle for a sandwich lunch in between pottering about with my paints and easel. Then one day I asked myself what was I doing mooning round the house all day. Why didn't I get in the car, drive to the Derby or Romanoff's – anywhere, so long as I could have a drink and see some human faces? So I jumped in the car and drove like blazes. I was just approaching Sunset Boulevard when suddenly the engine petered out. I had forgotten to fill her up. There was nothing for it but to leg it to the nearest petrol station, unless I could find a phone box and SOS for help.

I got out of the car and started walking. I kept stopping, trying to thumb a ride off a passing car, but there were no Good Samaritans about that day. A heat-wave was on and after the first mile I was outwardly sweating and inwardly swearing, when suddenly there came into view a broken neon sign announcing 'Barney's Beanery'.

Inside it was pitch-dark, save for the flickering lights from the fruit machines. Several juke-boxes were playing at full blast and I pushed my way through densely packed, swaying bodies to the bar, which was presided over by a man with a shock of white hair who wore his shirt open to the waist. I had to shout to make my request heard. 'Can I use your telephone?' I yelled. The giant behind the bar shook his long white locks. 'First you buy a drink. No one comes into Barney's without buying a drink.' 'What do you suggest?' I inquired. The giant grinned 'You look all in, buster. A "Doxey Daisy" would pick you up.' 'What's a "Doxey Daisy"?' I asked, thankful for a pause in the background racket.

'It's Barney's way of testing your drinking powers. It's lethal. Stick to Scotch,' came the reply from under a battered straw hat pulled down over the face of the man next to me, who was literally propping up the bar, or vice versa. I peered under the hat and saw, although it was unshaven and haggard, the unmistakable face of John Garfield. 'Forgive the intrusion, Mr Garfield,' I said hesitantly, 'but I would be honoured if you allow me to offer you a drink. You have always been one of my favourite actors.' He laughed sardonically and said 'When referring to me as an actor you ought to use the past tense.' I replied 'That's exactly how I'm beginning to feel.' He gave me a piercing look. 'You're a goddam limey, aren't you?' I nodded. 'New to this town?' I nodded again. 'Then let me wise you up,' he said with an effort at gaiety. Then turning to Barney he called, 'Set 'em up, Barney. Two Scotches for a couple of guys who feel like actors in the past tense.'

I was touched by his sincerity and found myself talking to him about my frustrations as I had talked to no one since my arrival in Hollywood. His wry comment hit the nail on the head. 'You'd better watch out or you'll be known as Mr Elizabeth Taylor!' He downed his drink, got unsteadily to his feet and, doffing his broken straw hat, said, 'Goodbye, limey. And don't let MGM eat you for breakfast.' Suddenly I felt I had found a kindred spirit. 'Just one more for luck, Mr Garfield?' I said. He shook his head. 'I outlived my luck long ago. I only drink to seek oblivion. Another drink and that old devil memory comes up and hits me in the guts.' And, so saying, he made his way to the exit.

Watching him go, Barney said to me 'There goes one of the bravest guys ever to hit this bullshit town.' I replied that I'd heard what had happened to him as a result of his opposition to McCarthy. 'It's not that I'm thinking of,' Barney corrected me. 'I'm talking about the night of the *Gentleman's Agreement* party. Everyone prefers to forget it now, but that night Johnny was a real hero. It never hit the headlines because he clammed up, but I heard the story from Gregory Peck's butler.'

It happened while America was still at war with Japan. Peck and Garfield had just appeared in *Gentleman's Agreement*. The story was of a gentile journalist who poses as Jew to investigate anti-Semitism in American society. The picture caused riots in several cities where it was shown and MGM itself was threatened when several hundred demonstrators marched up and down outside the studio gates waving banners bearing anti-Semitic slogans. Undeterred, Peck announced that he was throwing a party to celebrate the Hollywood première. But at the last minute Greg went sick with Asian flu – so, as his friend and co-star, John Garfield took over as host.

Champagne was flowing and around midnight most of the hundred or so guests were on cloud nine, when suddenly the drawing-room doors burst open and on the threshold stood three GIs, one of them waving a pistol and shouting 'Where's that fucking Yid, mister bloody Peck, who played at being a Jewboy in that mother-fucking film?' He tapped his pistol. 'I've got a little souvenir for him, been saving it all the way from Guatemala!'

The effect on the guests was like an electric shock. No one moved, except John Garfield, who stepped forward to fact the pistol-waving GI. 'Listen, young man,' he said quietly, 'you've got it wrong. Mr Peck is no Jew. If it's a true-blooded Yid you've been saving your bullet for, then I'm your man. John Garfield. Real name Garfunkel and you can't get more Yiddish than that.'

Though very drunk, the young GI was enough taken aback by Garfield's bravery to try to explain himself. 'You bloody Yids!' he raved. 'Living it up at home. Scoring with all the dames while my pals die in the jungle. What do you know about that? I bet you haven't a clue. You're just like the rest of them. You talk about freedom, but it's true-blooded Yanks like my pals who go out and die for it!'

At that moment, John's housedicks pounced on the group and one, seizing the pistol, yelled to the other 'Call the police!' 'Stop!' cried Garfield in a voice loud enough for all to hear. 'Nobody is calling the police. Perhaps you haven't been informed,' he went on quietly, 'but these three young gentlemen are my guests.' Then putting his arm round the three youths he said 'I think some black coffee is in order. After that you can tell one bloody Yid just what hell war can be.' He gestured to the silent guests. 'And', he concluded, 'I can promise you a captive audience.'

About two months after Barney told me this story my phone rang. It was Hecht. 'Garfield died this morning. The doctor said it was heart failure. Christ Almighty, if I've ever heard of death from a broken heart, this is it.' Garfield's death rated four lines in the *Hollywood Reporter*. I rang Hecht. 'It's outrageous,' I said. 'He was among the best actors this town has ever produced!' Hecht replied quietly 'You're a new boy here, but after this you should have learned that once you put up a black in this lousy town no one will stick their neck out for you. Not even when you are dead.'

All too soon I was to learn the truth of those words. Up till then I had never doubted that one day the phone would ring and it would be Jack Warner himself, or Goldwyn or Zanuck, offering me a part which lived up to their golden promises, but now I began to realise that I was living in a fool's paradise.

11
Hollywood Boomerang

'AT worst I accepted Hollywood with the resignation of a ghost assigned to a haunted house. I knew what you were supposed to think about it but I was obstinately unhorrified.' The words are Scott Fitzgerald's, not mine, but they are a true reflection of my state of mind two years after my arrival in the celluloid city. I still remained optimistic, but unlike Fitzgerald's hero I felt far from unhorrified when I finally discovered what the studio moguls had in store for me.

In 1952 Hollywood was still the film capital of the world and still run, as it always had been, like a slave city. The producers were dictators, the agents were ten-per-cent spongers, while the actors were treated like blancmanges, to be cast in any mould which suited the studios' policies. The contract, as well as directing your professional career, also included clauses governing your private life. Any hint of scandal or breach of moral code and your career could be ruined overnight.

The worst scourge of a contract artist's life was miscasting. In this respect Bette Davis will always be honoured as a sort of Joan of Arc who dared disobey orders to play a part unsuited to her talents. Warner Brothers put her on indefinite suspension and cancelled her salary. Bette fought back and sued Warners in open court. Not only did she receive substantial damages but she won reinstatement in her position as queen of Warner Brothers.

And type-casting could be just as bad. Paul Muni, for example, having done six prison pictures on the trot, walked into Jack Warner's office one day and said 'When are you going to let me out on parole?'

Just the same, in 1952, the Zanucks, the Warners, and Uncle Sam Goldwyn and all were beginning to feel the ground shake beneath their feet from the effects of a world-wide earthquake – television. In that year, a report compiled by exhibitors across the country disclosed the ominous fact that cinema audiences had fallen by as much as 50 per cent. The industry's reaction could be expressed in one ugly word, retrenchment. Whether you were a top executive or a mere clerk you could never be certain that yours would not be the next head to roll in the name of economy. A new phrase crept into the front-office vocabulary. Even at studios as large as MGM producers were talking about making 'big little pictures', by which they really meant 'cheap pictures'.

This gloomy gossip had little effect on me at the time. I suppose I was still buoyed up by the fanfare of publicity that had preceded my arrival. My only fear was, could I live up to expectations? MGM had stated publicly: 'We visualise Michael Wilding as an ideal player for sophisticated drawing-room comedies, the sort that Robert Montgomery and William Powell have played.' Hollywood's Bible, the *Hollywood Reporter*, quoted Jack Warner's remark that 'After viewing *Under Capricorn* and having seen his two English films *Spring in Park Lane* and *Maytime in Mayfair*, I go on record in saying that I believe Michael Wilding is the biggest romantic male discovery since Rudolph Valentino.' But Hollywood not only failed to live up to its golden-tongued promises; I never had even the ghost of a chance to fulfil them.

The first Hollywood tycoon I met was Jack Warner. He was sitting behind a tank-like desk, puffing a huge cigar. His opening remark was 'So your name's Wilding. What's your first name?' 'My friends call me Mike,' I replied.

Warner reached across his desk and, shaking me warmly by the hand, said 'Welcome to Warner Brothers, Mike.' He looked down at a file, then a sudden gleam of recognition appeared in his tiny, beady eyes. 'Of course! You're Liz Taylor's husband. It all comes back to me now. Understand you're something of a star in England.' He looked down at the file again and then cleared his throat. 'Quite a record you've rung up for yourself, young man. I'm afraid there's nothing suitable for you right now, but I thought it was about time we met. Don't worry, you'll be hearing from me. You want to know something, Mike?' I nodded. He got up and slapped me on the back. 'I think you're the biggest screen discovery since Madeleine Carroll, so put that in your pipe and smoke it!' With all due respect to the actress in question, I thought this was a bit of an anticlimax after his public comparison with Valentino. I would at least have felt better if he had got the gender right!

So much for Warner Brothers, I thought; that's one studio which is not exactly queueing up for my services. For six months now I had not heard from MGM and I knew enough about Hollywood to know that a suspended actor seldom gets a second chance. But a couple of months later I received a phone call from MGM's chief executive, Benny Thau. 'I want to see you right away,' said Thau. 'Get into your car and be here in fifteen minutes. I've got a hot property to offer you and when I say hot I mean hot!' Now Thau always spoke in a whisper. One comic said that when he spoke 'dust came out of his mouth'. His English was even more unintelligible over the phone than in real life and I thought I hadn't heard him correctly. 'But Mr Thau,' I said, 'I'm still under suspension, aren't I?' 'Never mind the legalities,' he whispered, 'get over here quick!'

I rushed up to the nursery where Liz was playing with baby Michael and broke the good news. Liz was unimpressed. 'The only three words he understands,' she said, 'are "Yes, Mr Thau." He'll talk you into some second-rate picture and make you believe it's *Gone with the Wind*. Take my advice, don't commit yourself till you've seen the script.'

Despite Liz's warning, I entered the sacred portals of MGM's executive offices with hopes – hopes which dwindled while I was kept cooling my curiosity for over an hour. At last the crisp, calm secretary spoke the magic words 'Mr Thau will see you now.' I was shown into an enormous office, big enough to be a boardroom. Thau was hunched over a desk and he was on the phone.

'Gimme Tracy,' he was saying. After a moment's pause it was apparent that no one could give him Tracy, so he rasped 'Gimme Crawford.' Apparently no one could give him Crawford either, because he clanked down the phone and turned to me. 'What are you doing here?' he asked. 'You sent for me, Mr Thau,' I replied. He mopped his brow and a broad grin came over his face. 'Thank God there's one employee who turns up when I want to see him.' Then, getting up on his two duck-like legs, he waddled over to me and put his arm round my shoulder. 'We're going to do you proud, Mike,' he whispered. 'Starring you opposite Crawford. Robert Taylor was going to play the part. But I've sold you to Crawford instead.'

I was called on to play the role of a blind pianist. 'How does one simulate blindness?' I asked the director the day before shooting began. I forget his name for, as it turned out, Joan Crawford as good as directed *Torch Song*. Anyway, the director gave me a blank look and said 'Don't ask me. Just play it by ear.' In fact, it was Miss Crawford who might have been blind, deaf and dumb, for she never spoke a word to me except 'Good morning' and 'Good night' throughout four weeks' shooting!

I learned what I was in for the first morning she walked on to the set. She was an hour late and the harassed director did not even get round to introducing us before I found myself in front of the cameras doing our first scene together, which called on me to wrap the lady in my arms and kiss her passionately. When the director called 'Cut!' I turned to her with a friendly smile remarking 'That's the first time I have ever kissed a lady without being introduced.' In reply, Crawford turned her back on me, walked off the set and went into a huddle with the director, leaving me standing there like some forgotten extra. The whispered conference over, the director strode over to me and said solemnly 'Miss Crawford says could you please move your shoulder a shade to the right, as you were blocking her profile?'

And that is how we continued for four weeks, with Crawford conveying her wishes to me via the director. I wondered what I had done wrong. Sensing my discomfort, the assistant director explained the mystery to me. 'Don't think it's anything personal. Crawford never speaks to her leading men. Don't ask me why. Perhaps she turned sour on actors after she and Fairbanks junior broke up. Your guess is as good as mine.' Well, I vowed never again to go through the experience of being La Crawford's leading man.

Incidentally, I worked out my own method of feigning blindness. I would fix my eyes at midpoint between myself and the camera. Years later, when I was living in Brighton, I was stopped one day in the street by a lady wearing the uniform of St Dunstan's staff. 'Oh, Mr Wilding,' she gushed, 'I so admired your performance in *Torch Song*. You were so realistic. I suppose you studied the blind at first hand?'

My next Hollywood venture, *The Egyptian*, in which I played Pharaoh, was for Twentieth-Century Fox. It was a prime example of miscasting and the script read like an Oriental version of *Boy's Own Paper*. I knew it would be a disaster from the word go, but another child was on the way and I could not allow myself the luxury of being put under suspension again for rejecting a role. Luckily my co-star was Peter Ustinov, who like me treated the episode as one long joke and who was to become a great friend.

The director of the picture was Mike Curtiz, whose English was very poor. On the second day of shooting, there I was in a long white nightgown with my face blacked, as were five hundred or so extras. We were supposed to be gazing out over the desert sands, but in fact were looking down at the bottom of the studio lot. Curtiz picked up the loudspeaker and yelled 'Action!', followed by the command 'The men in white turn to the left!' What he meant was 'the man in white', addressed to me only, but his accent was so heavy that the five hundred white-clad extras all turned left and ruined the shot.

But it was dear, brilliant, witty Peter Ustinov who made the filming tolerable. We were both scornful of our roles and our absurd costumes. One day, Peter said to me 'I'm fairly certain you are a salt cellar, and me, I am the pepper pot. What I'm not certain about is who is going to pour who out.' Midway through a dramatic scene with Peter his words suddenly came back to me and I broke up, ruined the scene and surely cost the production a couple of hundred extra pounds. 'If I would laugh at any mortal thing 'tis that I would not cry' certainly applied. After the first night even Stewart Granger had only this to say: 'I didn't recognise you, old chap. You looked like one of the Black and White Minstrels with a hangover.'

The Egyptian, and my performance in particular, received a deserved slating from the American press and the reception in England was even worse. Leonard Mosley in the *Daily Express* wrote: 'What is Hollywood doing to our poor Mike? They have blacked his face, dressed him in a nightshirt and provided him with unspeakable dialogue. What a waste of a great talent.'

Then, when I was still smarting like a whipped dog under the critics' lash, a fate even worse than a lousy movie befell me. My private life became the target of one of the two most feared females in town, gossip columnists Louella Parsons and Hedda Hopper. They were read by everyone from the lowliest extra to the studio chiefs. Not only did they make many stars' lives a misery, they often could and did ruin careers and break up marriages with their daily poison. One of the most notable of their victims was Charles Chaplin. During his twenty-five years in Hollywood barely a week went by without a public attack on his morals, his politics and his love life. Louella Parsons went so far as to call for his deportation as an 'undesirable alien'.

Louella's copy received nation-wide circulation since her boss was the newspaper tycoon William Randolph Hearst. When Hearst learned that Orson Welles's *Citizen Kane* was said to be based on his life, he issued orders to give the film the 'silence treatment'. So far as the millions of Hearst readers were concerned the picture never existed.

To my mind, Hedda Hopper was the most deadly wielder of the poison-pen technique, which was to print a malicious story about a star's private life regardless of fact or truth and then, when the victim protested, to write a sugar-sweet retraction. But mud sticks. The victim often wanted to sue for libel, but he or she was forbidden to do so by the studio because it was bad policy to fall out publicly with the press in case they panned future films.

One morning Humphrey Bogart rang me at the crack of dawn. 'Have you seen Hedda's column this morning?' he asked. 'No,' I said, rather crossly, 'I was still asleep.' 'Then nip downstairs and you'll get a rude awakening.' Hedda had given me top billing. Under a photo of Stewart Granger and me larking about on his boat, she had written the caption 'More than just friends?' When I went on to read her lead story, which was splashed over two columns, my eyes nearly popped out of my head. She had traced the history of my long-standing friendship with Granger, but in every line there was more than a hint that we shared a homosexual relationship. My immediate reaction was to laugh. What an allegation to make about two of the greatest womanisers in the business! Her story ended with the lurid implication 'One doesn't like to imagine what went on when this pair were living it up together on a yachting trip to the Riviera.'

David Niven was the first to pour ridicule on Hedda's story. In the evening edition of the paper he was quoted as saying: 'I can well imagine what was going on all right. The population of the South of France doubled overnight!'

But by that time I was in no mood for jokes. I called Stewart and announced that I intended to issue a libel suit in our joint names. 'Count me out, pal,' said Stewart. 'You might as well sue God. Anyway, the studio wouldn't permit it. Just remind me, next time we are photographed together in public, not to hold your hand!' I replied 'Sod the studio. If it's the last thing I do in this town I'm going to fight this battle and I'm going to win!'

I summoned my lawyer, who was equally pessimistic, but on my insistence that very same day slapped a libel suit on Hedda and the paper for defamation of character. A couple of weeks later I was the hero of Hollywood – the first person to stand up to the poison-pen sisters and win. I received an out-of-court settlement and an apology, which pleased me more than the money, in which Hedda admitted that she had written the piece 'in a malicious and wanton fashion with complete disregard of the plaintiff's feelings'. More than that, she agreed to delete the slanderous passages from her latest book.

Meanwhile, back at MGM, worse was yet to come. My career did not last long enough for me to suffer from type-casting – but as for miscasting! I was having lunch one day with Liz in the studio canteen when over the intercom came a voice. 'Will Mr Michael Wilding please report to Mr Benny Thau's office immediately.' I did not keep God waiting. As I have said before, Thau's English needed an interpreter and as usual he whispered rather than talked. When he first said it I thought I could not have heard right. 'Would you mind repeating that?' I asked. 'You start dancing ballet on Thursday,' he repeated. 'You can't be serious,' I said. 'I didn't call you in here for a joke session,' he replied icily. 'I'm casting you in *The Glass Slipper* opposite Leslie Caron. You play Prince

Charming.' 'You must be mad!' I protested. 'People start ballet when they are three foot tall, don't they?' 'I don't know and I don't care,' snapped Thau. 'You start on Thursday.'

Well, the production started on Thursday – but I did not. When I walked on the set the entire New York Ballet Company, headed by Roland Petit, was waiting for me. I had on a bowler hat and carried an umbrella as an act of defiance, just to show how unsuitable I was for my intended role. I went to the bar and did a mock *pas de deux*, umbrella and all, then I turned to Petit and said 'I can't do it, can I?' 'You mean you've never done any ballet before?' asked the startled Petit. 'Never danced a step in my life. Now, tell me the truth: can you see me in this role?' Petit looked shocked. 'Since you put it that way, my answer is frankly no.' 'Do me a favour,' I asked him fervently. 'Go and tell Mr Thau that.' Half an hour later, Petit returned, shaking his head. 'It didn't work,' he said; 'Thau says you're the only actor who can do it.' 'Do what?' I asked. 'Dance it,' replied Petit grimly.

There was nothing for it but to fall back on my ability to imitate. Petit was the very soul of patience and rehearsed me twelve hours a day. He gave me a crash course in ballet techniques, and with the sympathetic help of Leslie Caron I struggled through four of the most agonising weeks of my career. I made a fair pass at imitating dance steps, but I could not imitate muscles and the 'lifts' gave me a great deal of discomfort in my most tender parts. Petit advised me to wear a dancer's jockstrap. This only increased the agony. On the final day after doing my final 'lift' for the last shot of the film, I collapsed with Leslie on top of me. That same day I was called to take part in a publicity photo. I was still dressed, as I had been for the last scene, as a chef when I bumped into Lionel Barrymore in the corridor. Barrymore said 'Hello, Mike. I suppose it is you? You look like a milk bottle.' I felt more like a broken milk bottle, in fact.

I did not attend the première of *The Glass Slipper* and

did not dare look at the notices, except for a somewhat ironic review from a very highbrow American ballet magazine, sent to me by Petit, which read: 'We understand Mr Wilding is well known in Britain as a film star. But in view of the skill he shows as a dancer, it is difficult to believe that he has not, in earlier life, received expert tuition in the art of ballet.'

The only comfort to my wounded ego was that some of my early British films were being shown on television. At least, I comforted myself, a portion of the American public will not think I am a complete ass. However, at the same time the gossip columnists began insinuating that all was not well in my private life. No doubt out of revenge for my having sued her, Hedda Hopper was the first to print a direct attack. 'The Wildings fight like cat and dog,' she reported gleefully. To which accusation Liz retorted 'Of course we fight. It would be garbage to say we didn't. But that doesn't mean divorce.'

Louella Parsons struck nearer home when she wrote 'When they go out to parties, the Wildings have eyes for everyone but each other.' In a sense this was true, for Liz had such magnetism that she only had to enter a room for every male in sight to migrate in her direction. But then marriage had not exactly dimmed my eye for female beauty and rather than sulk and play the injured husband I used to enjoy the odd flirtation with such as Maria Montez or Marie 'The Body' McDonald. Humphrey Bogart ticked me off, saying 'You're always surrounded by the most beautiful babes at one end of the room, while Liz holds court with all the most attractive males at the other.' He wagged a warning finger at me. 'Married folk didn't ought to act that way.'

In fact, Hedda's allegation that we 'fought like cat and dog' wasn't strictly true. Our rows were one-sided. Liz had a quick temper, but I am basically placid. When she started to pick a quarrel, usually about something quite trivial, I used to infuriate her by refusing to be drawn into a ding-dong row. 'You're so goddam British!' she used to rage. 'I'll bet if I told you I'd taken a lover your only reaction would be to ask him round for afternoon tea!'

I remember one typical row. One habit of mine which used to annoy her was that immediately after breakfast I would sit down and do the *Times* crossword. One morning, she snatched the paper from my hand, tore it in half and threw it on the fire. 'So much for you and your stupid games,' she screamed, adding, 'Go on, hit me! Why don't you?' 'I've never gone in for hitting hysterical females,' I replied calmly. 'Oh God!' she moaned, 'if only you would. At least that would prove you are flesh and blood instead of a stuffed dummy!'

I was still in love with her, but I found the daily tremors of living with such a volcanic creature more and more difficult. Her temper apart, I was discovering other characteristics in my young wife which did not make for a harmonious relationship. I told Dick Sheppard: 'Liz has very little of the housewife about her. Forgetting to order dinner and things like that. She can't cook and shows no signs of trying to learn. She is untidy to the point of disaster. She makes a room look as if a tornado has hit it. It's a kind of disease with her. But her worst fault is her complete lack of sense of time. If we are going out to a party or première, she always starts to dress on time, then puts on a long-playing record and varnishes her nails. We never arrive anywhere on time. I tell you, it's hard to live with.'

To be fair to Liz, I was finding it increasingly difficult to live with myself. There is a saying in Hollywood: 'You're only as good as your last picture.' Not much comfort to an actor who knew he had made two stinkers in a row and whose Hollywood career had proved a definite non-starter. It was all very well to hear Liz complain that all the pictures she made between 1952 and 1956 were 'rubbishy' pictures, but to MGM her name was still synonymous with box-office gold while my status was that of box-office poison. I was not jealous of Liz's stardom, but I felt that my role in our marriage resembled that of the non-hero in *A Star is Born*. Not that I had taken to the bottle or had any plans for a heroic suicidal exit; just the same, I felt like a displaced person, strictly not wanted on the voyage.

Curiously enough, it was a high spot in Liz's career that brought about a temporary reconciliation. The film was *Giant*, which gave her a role worthy of her dramatic powers and was to win for her the greatest critical praise of her career to date. This and her next film also brought her into contact with two of the most brilliant actors of the decade, James Dean and Montgomery Clift. Both had rocketed to fame as symbols of an increasingly anti-establishment generation who openly thumbed their noses at convention. Both were actors for whom a golden future was predicted, yet both were to die tragically at an early age.

I first met James Dean when I went to visit Liz filming *Giant* on location in the Texas desert. Of course, the gossip hens leapt to the conclusion that my visit was that of a jealous husband, who believed their contention that a 'hot romance' was blossoming between Liz and Dean. Such rumours did not worry me. I had always borne in mind what Liz made a point of telling me even before we were married. 'Darling,' she had confessed, 'I can't help it but I always fall a little in love with my leading men. And I expect I always will. But it doesn't mean anything, I promise you. I know I have a lot of faults, but I have never two-timed any man and I never will. You have to believe that.'

I did believe her, although I knew that all her leading men also fell for her. Who can blame them? But I have never known any of them quite so frank about it as Dean. His words of greeting to me were 'You'd better know right away, Mike, that I have fallen madly in love with your wife!'

But the true reason for my visit to Texas location was an SOS from Liz. Apparently, Dean and the director, George Stevens, were always at loggerheads. 'They're always shouting at each other,' she complained, 'and I get caught in the crossfire. I thought perhaps as my husband you might act as referee. At least I'll have a shoulder to cry on.' Well, I performed the latter function between shots, but I wasn't able to do much refereeing between a brilliant director and an actor who was a law unto himself, as I found out on my first day on the set.

Dean was such a good actor that he would know instinctively if he had underplayed a line or overplayed a reaction, and he would break off in the middle of a scene, shouting 'Cut!' Such actions threw the camera crew into chaos and naturally affronted Stevens, who felt quite rightly that Dean was usurping his role as director. Stevens blew his top, but Dean would remain calm and come up nine times out of ten with a perfectly logical argument about how he could do the scene better in the next take. As a result the filming was one long feud between the two men and I could well understand Liz's frustration.

I have never known such vitality wrapped up in one individual. James Dean's confidence in his own judgement bordered on megalomania. He must have had a photographic memory and learned his part from fade-in to fade-out, for I never saw him look at the script. Instead, between takes he would be studying roles that he planned to play in the future; these included *Hamlet*, *Faust*, and every play ever written by Tennessee Williams. After a day's shooting in the hot sun the crew would return to the desert hotel utterly exhausted. Yet they would come to life as if by magic when Dean appeared on the scene and gave a one-man show, acting out the various parts he had been learning to a captive but captivated audience.

But if Dean worked hard he played even harder. In between films he used to take off on a five-day bender, dropping in at all the gambling casinos between Palm Springs and Las Vegas. The tales of fortunes won and lost over a gambling table or in a poker game were legendary. It was not only in games of chance that Dean was a

40　With Odile Versois in *Into the Blue* – the first and last picture I ever produced

41　Anna as Florence Nightingale and me as Sidney Herbert in *The Lady with a Lamp*

42   Anna, Herbert and me at the Royal Film Performance of *The Lady with a Lamp*

43   The three of us being presented to Princess Elizabeth and Lady Mountbatten

44 Liz at the Royal Film Performance of *The Lady with a Lamp* –
our first public appearance together

45 *Derby Day* – Anna and I as two strangers, who find they have
much in common

46 *Trent's Last Case* – me as the detective, quizzing Margaret Lockwood

47 Me, heavily disguised for *The Egyptian,* my first Hollywood fiasco

48   Breakfast with Liz

49   Liz and I spending an evening with our favourite Cole Porter records – and one of Liz's many pets

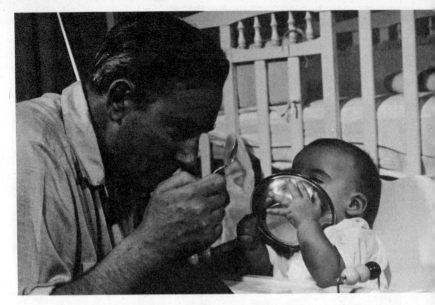

50   An interesting new role

51   Michael junior inspecting my portrait of Liz, while the subject looks on

52 Maggie, at the height of her career

53 My sketch of Maggie

55 Words of encouragement from Maggie during the filming of *Lady Caroline Lamb*

gambler: he frequently took his life in his own hands with his passion for fast cars. His most treasured possession was a Porsche roadster, which he drove at such reckless speed and with so little regard for the rule of the road that the Los Angeles police threatened to take away his licence.

As it was, the studio chiefs had banned him from driving during the production of *Giant*. His part was finished a week before the end of shooting and so the ban was lifted. The very next day he climbed into the Porsche and was driving at over a hundred miles an hour along Highway 99 when he lost control of the car, collided head-on with a truck and was killed instantly.

We were still at the Texas Hotel on location when the news of his death was broadcast on the radio. Liz was distraught with grief and made phone call after phone call hoping to learn that the news was not true. Finally, she got through to his doctor, who confirmed that Dean's body lay in the hospital mortuary. Even then, she refused to go to bed, but sat up weeping and crying 'I feel as though I've lost a dear brother.'

She was horrified when close on midnight she received a call from the production manager saying that Stevens would expect her to report for work the next morning to do her 'reaction' shots as arranged. 'The sod!' Liz raged. 'The heartless sod! He means my reaction shots to the last scene I did with Dean. He might as well expect me to do reaction shots to a corpse!'

Trooper that she is, Liz obeyed orders but she refused to talk to Stevens between shots. At the end of the day, she walked up to him, her eyes blazing. 'This is the last time I'll ever work for a goddam heartless ghoul!' she cried in a voice loud enough for the entire crew to hear, then she turned her back on him and walked off the set.

Montgomery Clift, who co-starred with Liz in *Suddenly Last Summer*, was unique among her leading men, being a self-confessed homosexual. But I was quick to notice that he followed Liz around like a lovelorn dog. 'It's no good trying to hide my feelings,' he confessed to me, 'I just can't get over it – Liz is the only woman I have ever met who turns me on. She feels like the other half of me.'

Withdrawn in manner, brilliant in intellect and at the top of his career, Monty was neverthless a man haunted by depression, but Liz in her magical way brought out the best in him on and off the screen. She told me 'I'm not in the least in love with Monty. But I love him as I would a lost child. He brings out the mothering instinct in me.' Strangely enough, he also brought out my own protective feelings when he said 'I'm the loneliest man in town. I've got plenty of dough, a lovely house, but no real buddies. When I get home after a day's shooting I find myself talking to the walls.' So, when Liz suggested that we invite him as a house guest for the remainder of the picture, I agreed.

The gossip queens were quickly writing about the Wildings' *'ménage à trois'*, with Monty in the role of 'the other man'. Nothing could have been further from the truth. Monty was at first a willing, but soon a wearied, go-between. Liz would cry on his shoulder during the day, while I would pour out my grievances far into the night after she had gone to bed. He acted as interpreter for two people who no longer spoke the same language, and must have got a clearer picture of the reasons for the breakdown of our marriage than anyone else in Hollywood.

Monty would try to explain Liz's point of view. 'She says you treat her like a child,' he told me. 'Try and remember that she is a mature woman and the mother of two children. Treat her as an equal. Despite your being older than she is she wants to be treated like a responsible human being.' In return I would list my complaints, which usually centred on a problem that neither of us could do anything about. That goddam age gap. I told Monty 'I feel I am nothing more to Liz now than a boring old appendage who can't even pull his weight as a breadwinner.'

My last memory of Monty is, I fear, a sad one and

prophetic of his equally sad end. By now, fed up with our daily confessions, he had moved back to his house in Malibu. But he was still a constant visitor, and when Liz decided to hold a party to celebrate her birthday Monty's name was at the top of the guest list.

The party had been going on for about four hours, but to Liz's great disappointment he had not shown up. It must have been past midnight when the doorbell rang. It was Monty. He looked desperately tired and was swaying slightly. 'Monty.' I cried, 'how are you?' 'None too gorgeous,' he replied. My heart sank, for I had grown to learn that this phrase signalled one of his depressive moods. Liz hugged and kissed him, but he refused her offer of a drink and went off to sit by himself in a corner. Seeing him alone, she immediately went over to him. 'Monty,' Liz pleaded, 'please don't look so sad. It's my birthday and I want everyone, most of all you, to be happy with me.' Monty brushed her aside and got unsteadily to his feet, saying 'You'll have to excuse me, sweetie. Not feeling too gorgeous, you understand.' With a grandiose wave of farewell to the rest of the guests he was making his exit when Rock Hudson, noticing Monty's glazed look, took his arm and said 'Time for me to pull the blinds down too.'

Liz and I both waved them goodbye at the front door and then rejoined our guests. It could not have been more than ten minutes later when we heard the doorbell ringing frantically, followed by the sound of someone hammering to be let in. White-faced, Rock stumbled over the threshold. 'For God's sake call an ambulance!' he cried. 'Monty's had a terrible accident. I think he's trapped inside his car.'

After calling an ambulance, Liz and I scrambled into Rock's car and set off at breakneck speed down the mountain road. We had gone about a quarter of a mile when suddenly we saw Monty's car – wrapped round a telegraph pole and teetering dangerously over the edge of the cliff. Liz screamed 'Come on, we must try and get him out!' She leaped from the car and, with the two of us vainly trying to keep up with her, scrambled over piles of boulders until she reached the wreck. Liz pounded on the side of the battered hulk calling out Monty's name. Meanwhile Rock, with great presence of mind, rushed back to his car, drove up, and turned his headlights on the wreckage.

Then we saw poor Monty. He was trapped in the front seat, his face covered in blood, moving his head from side to side and moaning like a wounded animal. I tried to force the driver's door open, but it was jammed, as were the two rear doors. Liz, like some demented creature, picked up a rock and bashed a hole through the window, and before Rock or I could stop her wriggled through the hole and reached Monty's side. Regardless of the fact that at any moment the wreckage might plunge over the cliff, she sat there cradling Monty's smashed face in her lap, wiping away the blood with the sleeve of her dress and saying over and over again. 'You're going to be all right, Monty darling. You're going to be all right.'

Someone must have tipped off the local press, for before there was any sign of the ambulance a car came screeching up the mountain road and stopped at the scene of the accident. Out jumped two men, one of them carrying a camera and flash-gun. 'We're from the *Los Angeles Examiner*,' explained the photographer. 'Just want to grab a shot of the victim.'

Now Rock is six foot four and I am six foot one. In one voice we both said 'Oh, no you don't!' and stood blocking their view. The frustrated newsmen swore at us and pleaded that they were only doing their job. 'Clift is hot news, front-page stuff,' said one of them. I could not help thinking how much greater their frustration would have been if they had known what the picture was that they had missed.

Miraculously, plastic surgery repaired Monty's broken face, but no one could make sense of the workings of his tortured mind. He had shot to stardom like a rocket, but was to vanish from the Hollywood scene as mysteriously as a ghost in the night. Rumour had it that in addition to taking to the bottle he had become a drug addict and four years later when he was found dead in a shabby New York hotel room the press immediately pounced on drugs as the cause of death. However, at the inquest the diagnosis was acute angina.

His last recorded utterance was reported from Las Vegas a year before his death, where apparently he was whiling away his time and his fortune at the gambling tables. Some local newshound spotted him and questioned him about his plans. Monty is said to have replied: 'I have two objects in mind. The first is never to step in front of a movie camera again in my life. The second, to try and find what has so far eluded me – a reason for living.'

12
Odd Man Out

IT was ironic and perhaps inevitable that Liz's
performances in *Giant* and *Suddenly Last Summer*,
which earned her critical acclaim as one of Hollywood's
finest actresses, should coincide with the end of our
marriage. We now had separate bedrooms and apart from
daily sessions with our children we seldom met. I retreated
to my study and Liz to her boudoir. When we did meet, our
conversation was an exchange of stilted politeness. I was
still in love with her, but a barrier of silence and rejection
had grown between us.

A trivial incident sparked off our parting. I was offered
Rex Harrison's role in a US tour of *My Fair Lady* and
turned it down flat. When Liz got to hear of it, she strode
into my study, flushed with anger. 'You're nothing but a
coward,' she blazed. 'To think that the man I once loved
turns out to be nothing but a coward!'

What I could not face at the time was that there was a
basis of truth in her accusation. After twelve years away
from the stage I feared that I lacked the stamina to face a
long-running tour, let alone to follow up Rex's triumph.
Liz's accusation had cut too deep and we had the row to
end all rows. In the end I packed my bags and called Joe
Cotten to ask if I could stay with him. My parting words to
Liz were 'Call me every day so I can talk to the children.
Try to understand we need a rest from one another. I'll
be back in a week or so.' But I think we both sensed

that we would never live together again as husband and wife.

Joe, bless his heart, turned out to be my Rock of Gibraltar, sitting up with me late into the night, while we talked about everything under the sun except my marriage and my career. True to her promise, Liz phoned every day, which gave me a chance to speak to the boys, and we agreed that I would visit the house every Saturday to keep up appearances in front of the kids.

Our attitude towards one another was one of guarded friendship. Our conversation was limited to the welfare of the boys. Divorce was never mentioned, but ironically enough it was during this separation that Liz first met the man who succeeded me as her husband.

A much-heralded newcomer to the town but already a legendary figure, even before he had made his first film, Mike Todd was in the process of hustling up finance for a film everyone said he would never get off the ground, *Around the World in Eighty Days*. Among the many stars he approached was Liz and, mostly out of curiosity, she accepted his invitation to have drinks with him on his yacht, where gossip had it he was ensconced with his latest girl-friend, Evelyn Keyes, ex-wife of John Huston.

As his invitation coincided with the day of my visit to the boys, Liz asked if she might bring us along too. My first impression was of the most dynamic personality I had ever met. Small in stature, Todd had the personality of a giant, oozed charm and was always cracking jokes. In retrospect, I suspect Todd fell for Liz the moment he set eyes on her. They seemed to bring out the best in each other. It had been a long time since I had seen Liz laugh, but after a few minutes in his company she was at her sparkling best, her mood matching Todd's wit and overflowing exuberance.

During the drive home, Liz was unusually quiet. 'What are you thinking about?' I asked. 'That extraordinary man. He's like a character straight out of *The Arabian Nights*.' 'Never read it,' I replied. 'Neither have I,' she said, 'but I always imagined it was about men who could get anything they wanted once they'd set their hearts on it. That's Mike Todd for you.'

Soon after that I received an ominous phone call from Liz. I knew by her tone that she had something more on her mind than an exchange of small talk about the boys. 'You sound sad,' I remarked. 'Anything I can do to help?' 'Yes,' came her prompt reply. 'Can you be your usual darling understanding self and bear with me and listen to a statement I've just written? It's for the press making our separation official, but I'd like you to hear it before it's published.' 'Thanks,' I said, 'but I'd rather just read it in the papers, then I can believe it's about two other people.' 'Oh, Mike,' she cried, on the edge of tears, 'I still love you. I'll always love you. But it isn't ring-a-ding-ding any more. Do you understand?'

I understood only too well, particularly as the gossip columns were full of rumours about her whirlwind courtship with Mike Todd, which appeared alongside the headlines about our separation. Liz had written: 'It is being done so that we will have the opportunity to work out our personal situation. Much thought has been given to this step we are taking and we are in complete accord in making this amicable decision.'

We resumed our telephone talks but the ugly word 'divorce' was never mentioned, although we both knew it was inevitable. Six days after our separation notice I received a call from Liz's lawyer announcing Liz's intention to file divorce papers immediately on the grounds of mutual incompatibility, with the rider that I was to be allowed reasonable access to my children whenever I wished. She waived all her rights to alimony.

Three days later a decree nisi was awarded to Liz by the Los Angeles County Court. She hadn't phoned me that day and the first I knew about it was through reading the headlines in the evening paper. I put down the absence of her daily phone call to sensitivity on her part, but when two days went by and I still hadn't heard from her I tried to phone her. The phone was answered by her housekeeper, who told me that Miss Taylor had gone away for a short holiday. I had just put down the receiver, when Joe came in and strode straight across to the television and switched it off. I saw at once that something was wrong. He shuffled his feet and could not look me in the eye, then finally he blurted out 'Sorry to be the bearer of not exactly good news. But I'd rather you heard it from me first. Liz and Mike Todd were married this morning.'

Our divorce was only three days old. I gasped 'I just don't believe it!' Joe produced a copy of the evening paper he had been hiding behind his back. The picture on the front page jumped out at me – a radiant Liz, flowers in her hair, clinging to Todd's arm. The caption described how the couple had been married that morning at the City Hall and had left for an unknown destination for their honeymoon. I should have seen it coming, but as it was I felt as if I had been hit below the belt. All I could say was 'Don't you think Liz might have had the consideration to let the funeral meats grow cold?'

Joe sat up through the night with me and we ended up getting good and drunk. The next morning, soon after we woke with hangovers we both deserved, the phone rang. I staggered over to answer it and, holding the receiver to my throbbing head, heard an icy female voice inquire 'Is that Mr Wilding?' 'I think so,' I mumbled. 'Hold the line,' commanded the voice, 'Mr Benny Thau wants to speak to you.'

The mere mention of what for me had become a dreaded name sobered me up in an instant. Thau came straight to the point. He had a role lined up for me in a new production due to start shooting the following Monday. He then went on to issue the somewhat unsettling information that so far the picture had no title, no director, and the script was still being written. 'But,' he concluded, 'such matters are my concern. Just see you haul yourself over here next Monday at eight o'clock and you'll have no worries.'

'But wait a minute, Mr Thau,' I stammered. 'I do have a worry – an urgent worry and a request. I'd like to see the script before making a decision.'

There was a gurgling, choking sound from the other end of the line like a man having an apoplectic fit, but finally he managed to spit it out. 'Actors don't make decisions in my studio. They obey orders, my orders. And I'm telling you if you fail to report for work at eight o'clock Monday next you'll be breaking your contract.'

I turned to Joe in despair. 'It will only be another disaster. What shall I do?' Joe replied drily 'You'll do what the rest of us do, obey orders. I'll keep my fingers crossed for you. This might turn out third time lucky.'

Such hopes were dashed the next morning when an MGM messenger delivered the pages of my opening scene. So far as I could gather, what I had let myself in for was another dreary rehash of the Old Errol Flynn-type pirate picture. As usual there was a baddy pirate and a goody pirate, and I was to play the latter. My last and only memory of that picture was sitting down on the Sunday before shooting began, gritting my teeth and trying to learn unspeakable lines. I cannot remember the name of the director, the name of the picture or even if it ever saw the light of day. It was the first time in my screen career that an ailment which had troubled me for many years affected my performance. I just could not get the lines into my head and arrived for the first day's shooting with a completely blank mind and a raging headache. When the cameras started to roll and the director called 'Action!', I found I could not utter a word. 'Haven't you learned your lines?' asked the director. 'Yes and no,' I replied truthfully. He must have been a kind as well as a patient man, for all he said was 'You don't look a hundred per cent. Aren't you feeling well?' 'None too grand, I'm afraid,' I murmured. He patted me on the shoulder. 'Not to worry,' he said with false cheerfulness, 'we'll shoot round you this morning. Go to your dressing-room and have a good sleep. You'll be all right this afternoon.'

But the afternoon arrived and the lines still didn't come. Finally the now harassed director arranged for cue boards with my lines to be set up in front of the camera. Even this did not work as by now I was overcome with another familiar symptom – double vision. The poor director did what any director would have done in the circumstances. He called off shooting for the day. But, unlike most directors, he remained sympathetic to an actor obviously, if mysteriously, in distress. 'See you tomorrow. I'm sure you'll be feeling better,' he comforted me. Then he added, with a hangdog expression 'But you do understand, I shall have to report this to head office or my neck will be on the chopping-block.'

I drove home, went straight to bed and slept for fourteen hours. The next morning I woke up completely refreshed. My head was as clear as a bell. I could recite my lines by heart and set off for the studios feeling on top of the world. As I drove through the studio gates, the commissionaire signalled me to stop. 'Morning, Mr Wilding. I have an urgent message for you. Mr Thau said that as soon as you arrived I was to tell you to report at once to his office.' I accepted the message with the nonchalance of a schoolboy about to receive a ticking off from the headmaster. However, I felt a slight chill of apprehension when the icy-voiced secretary, instead of asking me to wait in the outer office as usual, sprang to her feet at my entrance and announced with a look of disdain on her usually implacable face 'Mr Thau is waiting for you.'

He was seated behind his desk, engulfed as usual by a cloud of cigar smoke, opening his morning mail. 'Good morning, Mr Thau,' I said, sounding more cheerful than I felt. 'I hear you wanted to see me.' Without even looking up from his mail, he grunted 'I hear you held up a day's production because you hadn't learnt your lines.' 'I'm sorry, Mr Thau,' I said, 'I'm afraid I wasn't feeling too well.' For the first time he looked up at me and, gesturing with his paper knife, he rasped 'This is a film studio. Not a hospital ward.' Then he swiftly opened his desk drawer and took out a document, which he waved under my nose. With a trembling voice he asked, 'Do you see what this is?'

'It looks like my contract, Mr Thau,' I replied.

'Right first time. Now may I remind you that there is no clause in that contract that requires this studio to continue employing an actor who cannot learn his lines.' And, so saying, he snatched the contract from my hands, tore it in half and threw it into the wastepaper basket.

'But, Mr Thau,' I pleaded, 'I sometimes get these bouts. Not in twenty years of filming have they ever interfered with my work. I'm all right now and word-perfect. Surely you'll give me a second chance?' Thau picked up his paper knife, pointed it at me like an accusing dagger and replied. 'In this town actors don't get second chances. Do I have to spell it out for you? You're fired!'

The ignominy of my exit from MGM was made public for all to read in the next day's press with such headlines as 'Famous British star fired for not learning lines'. The first and only spoken word of sympathy I received was a phone call from Liz. 'It's a scandal!' she raged. 'You must appeal at once against unfair dismissal.' 'Alas, there was nothing unfair about it,' I replied. 'Actors who can no longer learn their lines are like carpenters who can no longer saw wood. They deserve to be axed.'

Now a publicly black-listed actor, I began to realise how John Garfield must have felt. But I understand only too well my fellow actors' reaction. To them I had become a symbol of failure, an object of embarrassment, so they took the easy way out and shunned me. Apart from the daily calls from Liz, my phone stopped ringing. Even my agents put up a blockade of silence, which was hardly surprising as they were the biggest outfit in town, with all the star names on their books. What hope had they of earning their ten per cent from a black-listed actor?

Joe Cotten remained loyal, bless him, but I decided that if I stayed with him any longer I would be like a man who came to dinner. So I found myself a two-roomed apartment on Sunset Boulevard. An appropriate address, I told myself. As days merged into weeks, I found myself living more and more the life of a recluse. I had even given up for the time being my weekly visits to my children since I did not feel up to meeting face to face the man who had replaced me as Liz's husband. I felt like a juggler who had had the mats pulled out from under him. My marriage had failed and my Hollywood career had ended in disgrace. I shunned old haunts for fear of embarrassing encounters with old friends. I half-heartedly filled my day with reading and dabbing at painting, ate out at the nearest delicatessen and wandered back each night to an empty apartment, a bottle of vodka my only companion.

Then the last thing in the world I had expected happened in what I felt to be a friendless town. Jerry Hogan, one of the most successful independent agents in town, who unlike the majority of his calling was respected by actors and studios alike, asked me how I would feel about joining him as a partner?

'Thanks for the compliment, Jerry,' I replied, 'I could hardly wish to work for a nicer guy. But I can hardly see myself in the role of an agent. Too soft-hearted.' Jerry reeled off a number of reasons why I was wrong. He said that having been an actor myself I would have the advantage of knowing how clients react. He said I would be able to understand their fears and their hopes and I would be able to guide them and give them confidence. 'As for talent-spotting,' he concluded, 'remember that story you told me about the girl in the chorus?'

He was referring to an incident in the early fifties when I was still working for Herbert Wilcox. I had spotted an exceptionally pretty girl in the front row of the chorus of a topical revue. The same night I went backstage and met her. I was immediately smitten, but was also sure that here was star material in the making. So I arranged a meeting with Herbert. She was shaking with nerves, so much so that I had to push her into Herbert's office. Ten minutes later she emerged from the interview near tears.

Apparently, Herbert had offered her a contract as a small-part player.

I stormed angrily into his office, saying he had insulted the girl by only offering her half the salary she was getting as a chorus girl. Herbert allowed me to finish letting off steam, then with a twinkle in his eye he said 'As usual Mike, where a pretty girl is concerned, you're letting your heart rule your judgement. In a month's time you will have forgotten her name.' But I was never to forget her name and Herbert was to experience regret when six months later the girl was offered a Hollywood contract and shot to stardom in *Roman Holiday*. The girl was Audrey Hepburn.

Anyway, as a result of Jerry's charm and persuasion, I eventually accepted his offer and became a Hollywood agent. At first I found my new role challenging, even enjoyable, as I was being given a chance to meet on the most intimate terms many big stars who to my surprise seemed willing to put their careers in my inexperienced hands. But, when it came to talking money and contracts with the studio bosses, I fear I was miscast.

Finally Jerry, who was as shrewd as he was kind, sensed my unease and suggested a division of labour. He would handle the business side while I would act as front-man, meeting the artists and listening to their problems about their work and private lives. This arrangement seemed to work, no doubt because our clients were flattered at not being treated solely as the source of a ten per cent commission, but instead were greeted as friends by an odd Englishman who seemed to care about their welfare as human beings. It was through one of her typical acts of sympathy that Liz became a client. So, ironically enough, did Richard Burton. But they never met through us, at least so far as I know.

I shall always be grateful to Jerry, for it was two of our most famous clients who in different ways helped me to make a decision that I should have been able to make for myself. A tingle went up my spine when Groucho Marx entered my office. He was just as I'd seen him on the movies – that stalking walk, the enormous cigar, the huge horn-rimmed glasses and the twang to his voice when he announced what was to me shock news. He, along with his brothers, had decided to quit Hollywood and return to a stage career on Broadway. The Marx Brothers were then at the peak of their Hollywood fame and I expressed some puzzlement over their decision.

Groucho leaned over my desk and drawled 'I like the way you speak. I like the way you look. I think you might even understand what I'm going to say.' He took a long pull on his cigar and began pacing the office, talking all the while. 'You see, brother, I mean my brother in spirit of course, you understand?' I nodded. 'Well,' Groucho continued, 'if I've ever been anything it's an ad-lib comedian. A God-given ad-libber. When I first came to this cranky town, the directors were always insisting that I stuck to the script or they would shout "Cut!" Now, seeing that I took no goddam notice of either of these admonitions, they started to fool me. They would keep the camera running until I was fresh out of ad-libs. Then I go to my first première. And what do I find? The boys with the scissors had been at work and all my best ad-libs lay on the cutting-room floor. For eight years now, I have felt like a castrated ad-libber and I said to myself, just stick it, man, till you've made your pile, then you can go back to being the best ad-libber in the business, and kiss this town goodbye. But before I go I'm going to get my own back on a certain type of human reptile all too common in this town. You and Jerry are to be in on the joke because you both fit into that very rare status in Hollywood, gentlemen.'

Still pacing my office floor, but overcome with fits of maniacal laughter, he outlined his plan. He was going to throw a farewell party on his yacht. Ninety per cent of the guests, who were fellow stars, would receive an ordinary invitation. But the other ten per cent, into which Groucho lumped producers and agents, would receive instructions: 'The Marx Brothers announce a fancy-dress farewell party. All guests are requested to come dressed as pirates.' Groucho's parting words to me were 'Be sure and come to the party and see if those thick-skinned pirates get the message.'

Well, wearing conventional evening dress, I duly arrived at the party. You should have seen the look on Goldwyn's face when, in full pirate kit, he saw Zanuck, Harry Cohen, Uncle Jack Warner and all, also dressed up as pirates. Then followed the top agents, some of them even sporting cutlasses. Being birds of a feather, the unfortunate victims of Groucho's joke found themselves huddled together at one end of the boat while Groucho's other guests, trying to contain their laughter, romped at the poop end.

Around midnight Groucho called for silence and delivered a farewell speech as only Groucho could:

'Fellow infidels, in a few more hours I shall happily shake from my feet the dust of this misnamed madhouse known as "The City of Angels". If anyone among you starts to sing "Should Auld Acquaintance Be Forgot", I cannot say I echo your sentiments, but I warn all that if you do I will either have you thrown overboard or sent on long-term imprisonment to Repulsive Pictures. So the lawyers can be quite clear to whom they should address their libel suit, perhaps I should say Republic Pictures. Accustomed as I am to public speaking, I shall make my remaining remarks brief but abrasive. True, I shall miss some old familiar faces, but to those among you who have had the nerve to turn up at my farewell party dressed in their true roles as a bunch of money-grabbing pirates I will issue my official farewell in the form that you have always issued my contract. In triplicate.' And, so saying, he reached out and grabbed his two brothers and between the three of them they issued a raspberry loud enough to echo from MGM to RKO.

Groucho's farewell had given me pause for thought. But it was another famous client of ours, Edward G. Robinson, who was to make me decide that I did not belong in Hollywood. The first thing he did when he walked into my office was to go over and gaze at a Pissarro landscape which Liz had returned to me. 'Does that picture belong to you or to the establishment?' he asked. When I replied that it was my most precious possession, he stalked up to me with that familiar stiff gangster gait and put both his arms around my shoulders. 'To think', he exclaimed, 'I have found in this desert of a city, a man who appreciates art as I do.'

Now I knew that Robinson had accumulated one of the finest private collections of paintings in the country and found myself deep in conversation with him about art, even telling him about my early days as a student. It was only reluctantly that I pulled myself together and returned to business by suggesting we talk about the reason for his visit, namely the renewal of his contract with Warner Brothers.

Robinson made one of his famous grimaces. 'Who wants to talk contracts with a guy who knows a Van Gogh from a Picasso?' he cried. Then, jumping up on his stubby legs, he grasped my hand. 'Why not come up to my place for lunch?' he asked. 'Then afterwards I could show you my collection. None of the locals know the difference between a Renoir nude and a pin-up calendar. I would appreciate the opinions of an expert like you.'

Edward G. lived high up in the Hollywood hills above Topanga Canyon in an enormous, badly faked up New-England-style house. But there were no fakes in his collection, which occupied the four walls of a palatial panelled room and was obviously worth a fortune. But he still felt his collection was incomplete and told me 'I shall only continue working long enough to earn enough dough to travel Europe and pick up some missing treasures, you know, like the odd Renoir, my favourite Turner, my missing Pissarro. That done, I shall retire and, believe me, the only pictures I'll ever want to see for the rest of my life are those I can see within the privacy of these four walls.'

Enchanted as I was to find myself surrounded by so many famous pictures, I reminded myself that I had a job to do and reluctantly once again brought the conversation round to the problems about his contract.

Robinson's mouth curved down in that familiar grimace and he almost shouted at me 'Contract? Leave that to your partner. What in hell's name is an artistic guy like you doing wasting your time on piddling details like contracts? What did you say your moniker was?'

When I told him, his jaw dropped and a light of understanding dawned in those heavy-lidded eyes. 'Say!' he exclaimed, 'you're that poor limey actor who got the works from MGM?' I nodded. He paused for a moment then asked the direct question. 'And now do you see yourself as an agent? I can't believe it. You're too much of a gentleman.'

'I don't know about the gentleman,' I replied, 'but you're right not to believe in me as an agent. I don't believe in myself.'

He mused for a moment, then said 'You seem like a guy in need of some advice.' I nodded. 'Well, on the basis of our short acquaintance, would you think it presumptuous if I said I'm the guy who could give you the right advice?' 'I think it's very generous of you to be concerned about me,' I replied. He slapped me on the back. 'Right. But first we both need a drink.' He led me out of the gallery to an impressive bar with windows looking out on the Pacific. 'Being a limey, you'd like a Scotch?' suggested Robinson. I nodded. 'And being a desperate limey you'd like a double?' Again I nodded my head. He poured us both something more like a triple Scotch, handed me my glass, and asked abruptly 'So you still want to hear my advice?' I did.

'I hear tell you were a big star in England,' he said. 'I also know that Hollywood has treated you shamefully. But that isn't the purport of my message, which is to tell you, whether you have realised it or not, that your arrival coincides with the death throes of Hollywood. Already, great talents are rebelling against the tyranny of the studio tycoons, going to France, to Germany, to timbuctoo – any place that will give them their own say in the parts they play and a cut in the profits. Two years from now and television will have taken over and be making rubbishy films on the back lots where Garbo used to tread and Gene Kelly sang.' He drained his glass, took a deep breath and looking me straight in the eye said bluntly 'Don't wait to see the death throes. Get the hell out of this goddam town and go back home to where you belong. Go anywhere, just so long as you rejoin the human race!'

This last phrase haunted me that night as I tried to get to sleep. I got up with my decision made. Sadly I broke the news to Jerry. 'Kind as you've been to put up with me,' I explained, 'I don't belong in Hollywood. I must go home. Do you understand?'

To my surprise Jerry bounced up at the announcement like a rubber ball and came out with a new proposition. He had always felt he needed a representative in Europe, someone who would be based in England, but could also visit the Continent in search of new talent. 'All I ask of you', he concluded, 'is that you return to Hollywood once a year so we can discuss progress and map our future plans. How does that hit you?'

I replied that it struck me as a typically generous gesture, but I was unsure that I could fulfil the demands of such a partnership and questioned his faith in me as a star-spotter. To which Jerry replied 'Just try it for one year. You have nothing to lose.' Indeed, I had everything to gain. Most important my self-respect, not to mention a generous and urgently needed salary.

A week later, as I glanced from the plane and spotted the familiar outline of the white walls of MGM, I asked myself if I had any regrets about the failure of my Hollywood career. My reaction was one of anger rather than sorrow or self-blame. I recalled Herbert's warning: 'You will never understand Hollywood, because Hollywood will never understand you.' He was right.

So much for the failure of my career, but what about the failure of my marriage? I realised that in a way both were connected and I recalled how John Clements and his wife had been opposed to my marrying Liz. 'Why?' I had asked at the time. 'What have you got against Liz?' John replied for both of them when he said 'Marriage to Liz will also mean your professional marriage to Hollywood and Hollywood will never understand you or appreciate your talents.' I looked back in anger rather than regret on a career that never was, but as for the break-up of my marriage, that I regretted.

13
Strange Interlude

M Y return to England was in bleak contrast with my departure six years previously. If I had left Hollywood as a black-listed actor, I returned to England as a forgotten one.

I moved into a rented Mayfair flat and more or less locked my front door on the world. It was a furnished flat and the only mementoes of my past were my own paintings, including a not very good life-size portrait I had made of Liz during our engagement. Try as I would, I could not entirely lock out her face from my memory. Two weeks went by and, apart from the friendly arrival of the char each morning, I did not see or speak to a soul. Every time I picked up the phone to talk to an old friend, something stopped me from dialling the number. I felt friends must have lost contact with me as I had with them.

In retrospect, I am sure I was shying away from reappearing as a failure on the scene of my successes. As for fulfilling my obligations as Jerry Hogan's partner, I could not face going out to the theatre or cinema alone. And for the first time in my life I had no feminine company on which I could rely. Nor did I desire it.

For a month I barely set foot outside the flat. Even sleep eluded me. The sleeping pills prescribed for me by the doctor did not seem to work. He said he would send me a prescription for something stronger, adding the warning that I should take no more than the prescribed dose and not mix them with over-much alcohol, or the result could be lethal.

It was growing dark when I arrived back at the cold, empty flat from my visit to the chemist. I took the pills out of my pocket, placed them on the table beside me, poured myself a strong vodka and repeated the process several times. Then I turned on the radio – to a voice that reminded me that it was St Valentine's day, the anniversary of my engagement to Liz. The coincidence triggered a thought which flashed through my mind like some remote message. It was as though some strange voice inside my head was saying 'Look, there's a solution to all your misery in that bottle of pills and the remains of the vodka.'

Suddenly I was stone-cold sober, but so shocked that I jumped to my feet, snatched up the bottle of pills and emptied them down the loo. Next morning I rang to make an appointment with Dr Henry Rowan, a doctor well known for sorting out the problems of show-business people. Rowan started off by assuring me I was not unique. Many of his patients, with far less cause than I, admitted to thoughts of suicide from time to time. He said I was suffering from delayed shock.

'It's hard enough for most people to cope with one tragedy in their lives,' he explained, 'let alone a double dose. I'm afraid I can't offer any immediate cure. Only another doctor can help you. His name is Time.'

Rowan's parting advice was to pick myself up and start working. That way I would regain my self-respect and he urged me to see old friends, who probably wanted word from me as badly as I wanted it from them. Well, the next night I made the effort and went to the West End opening of a new play. I arrived at the theatre rather late and the curtain had already gone up as I fumbled my way to the only seat vacant in the front row of the stalls. Trying to concentrate on the figures on the stage, I glanced neither to the right nor left of me. When the lights went up for the interval, an imperious voice sounded in my left ear.

'Excuse me, but I think you are sitting on my programme.'

I turned to face the voice and recognised its owner instantly. It was Dame Edith Evans. I got up, bowed and returned her programme. Then, to my amazement, a smile lit up her face. 'Why,' she exclaimed, 'if I am not mistaken, you are Mr Michael Wilding?'

I was astonished that she should remember me from Gibraltar and a single meeting some five years before. Herbert had been considering casting her in the title role in a film based on the life of Lilian Baylis, founder of the Old Vic. I happened to be having a drink in Herbert's suite at Claridges when she arrived. No one could fail to class Dame Edith as one of the greatest actresses of the century, but no one would ever describe her as a beauty in the classical sense of the word. Indeed, taken feature by feature, she was plain. Yet the moment she walked into the room I felt I was looking at a face illumined by an inner light which transformed her features into a beauty all her own. Herbert suggested that, since she had begun her career at the Old Vic, rather than play Lilian Baylis why should she not portray herself, which would give her the opportunity to re-enact some of her own great triumphs, such as Rosalind in *As You Like It*?

Dame Edith pondered the suggestion deeply, then shook her head and said 'No, Mr Wilcox, I could not do it. And I will show you why.' Whereupon she sprang up from the couch and, striding the floor of the room as if it were a stage, began to speak, not in the sonorous voice with which she had greeted me but in the timbre of a young girl, Rosalind's famous soliloquy of thwarted love.

I could not believe my eyes or ears. She must at that time have been in her middle fifties, yet her every move, word and gesture was that of a young girl. Then suddenly, breathlessly, her body limp from effort, sinking down on the couch, she cried 'Do you see what I mean? I can be sixteen again. But only for a moment. I could never recapture the semblance of youth long enough to sustain a screen performance.'

This evening I kissed her hand and, seeing that like myself she was alone, I asked whether I might escort her to the bar for some refreshment. 'Why,' she cried in that imperious voice, 'don't tell me you haven't some fair lady awaiting your company?' I shook my head and she made a sort of tut-tut noise. 'Where are all your beauteous females, Mr Wilding?' she inquired. 'That was a long time ago,' I replied, 'but if you will permit me to escort you to the bar I shall again be in such company.'

When I managed to get through the bar scrum and return with her tomato juice, she asked me point blank 'Where have you been hiding all these years?' 'In Hollywood,' I replied, hoping that she would change the subject, but she persisted. 'And what happened to you in Hollywood?' 'Everything and nothing,' I replied, and again tried to change the subject. Undeterred, she continued cross-examining me and I found myself telling her my reasons for not wanting to talk about Hollywood.

By the time I had finished, the bell was ringing for the second act and I got to my feet. Dame Edith put a restraining hand on my arm and asked simply 'Are you as bored with this play as I am?' I said 'I'm afraid so!' She burst out laughing. 'Why be afraid? Now you have no excuse, have you?' 'An excuse for what?' I stammered. 'Come on!' she cried gaily, 'What are you waiting for? Surely you're going to invite me out for dinner?'

From then on, she was in charge. The choice of the restaurant, the Ivy, was hers, as was the subject of the conversation, namely my future. I tried to dissuade her but she bore down on me as relentlessly as a battleship. 'If I'm not mistaken,' she declared, 'your life needs a helping hand. Some guidance. Some assurance. Am I right?' I nodded miserably. 'Well, I think I'm destined to be your adviser. We didn't meet tonight just by chance. Let me explain what I mean.'

She went on to tell me some facts about her own life. As well as being a practising Christian Scientist, she had discovered she had the gift of clairvoyance. 'Not that I have ever been able to predict my own future.' she admitted, 'but many times have I been able to do so for my friends. I'm not going to ask you the month you were born, I've never believed in all that rubbish about the stars, but I think I have learned enough about you to give a rough indication of your future.'

She told me that my tribulations were far from over. I would have yet another test of endurance ahead of me. But finally, if I would only be patient, I would meet a woman who would bring me lasting happiness in marriage, which she felt was my ultimate goal in life and took precedence over my career. I had to agree with her. As for her prophecies, they all came true. I was about to enter another period of upheaval which, ironically enough, only began as a result of the re-entry into my life of Liz and Mike Todd.

By now I had begun to try to earn my salary as an agent. I visited theatres all over the country and never missed a West End opening night. One such night in the theatre bar I heard a familiar voice shrieking, 'Mike! Darling Mike!' The next thing I knew I was being hugged and kissed. It was Liz, with Mike Todd. It was a complete surprise. I did not even know they were in England, as there had been none of the usual hullabaloo in the press and they had in fact only touched down at Heathrow a couple of hours earlier.

They bombarded me with questions. Had I been seeing old friends? Was I thinking of going back into films? Was I enjoying being home again? I avoided giving direct answers by saying that I was still trying to find my feet in a new role. Mike Todd slapped me on the back. 'What you need is someone to organise you, old chum, isn't that right?' To which I had no answer.

So I was not surprised when first thing next morning Todd was on the phone with an invitation to join him and Liz at a party to be given that night by a rich friend of theirs. 'We won't take no for an answer, Mike. If you don't come, Liz will mope. You wouldn't want that, would you?' He did mention the hostess's name, but I forgot it. So that night, in a 'what have I got to lose' mood, I arrived at the party.

It was like a rugger scrum. Liz and Mike were holding court at one end of the room and, as I didn't want to get mixed up in the mêlée, I picked up a drink from one of the knee-breeched butlers and retreated into a corner. As a result, at midnight, I watched the Todds leaving without having been introduced to my hostess. Most of the other guests had left too and I was still guzzling champagne in my corner when I looked up to see standing beside me a tall attractive blonde, who resembled a Cartier model. Diamonds blazed across her shapely bosom like a shining breastplate. She held a bottle of champagne in her hand and said 'How about one for the road, Mr Wilding?'

I was so startled that I simply nodded. 'Here's to my favourite film actor,' she said. It seemed that she had seen every film I'd ever made, including my Hollywood flops, about which she was sincerely indignant. 'Hollywood crucified you,' she said. Naturally such remarks were music to my ears. Now, I always wake up around about midnight and was grateful for the company of someone who was quite as wide awake as myself. She told me she had been married twice and was recently divorced and was feeling very unhappy about it. 'That puts us in the same boat,' I said. 'Perhaps we are not meant for marriage.' 'Oh, I wouldn't say that,' she retorted, 'I think it's just a question of finding the right partner.'

When a butler came into the room and asked if Madam would care for bacon and eggs, I at last realised that I had been talking to my hostess. Thoroughly chagrined, I apologised for not even knowing her name. She laughed. 'I'm glad. Most men have ulterior motives for seeking my company, if you see what I mean.' I did not see what she meant at all, but I was to learn soon enough. After tucking into the bacon and eggs and noticing that it was already getting light, I apologised for having outstayed my welcome. She replied simply 'You will always be welcome in my house.' Then she wrote down something on a paper napkin and handed it to me. 'Susan Nell's the name. I've written it down so this time you won't forget. Along with my telephone number.'

Around noon next day the phone rang. It was Susan inviting me to her house for supper. I said yes, because I couldn't think of any reason to say no. Then I rang Liz and asked her to tell me about Susan. Liz's response almost had me married by proxy. She raved about what a wonderful personality, such charm, so affectionate, the perfect mate for a lonely divorcee like myself. 'Of course,' she added as if as an afterthought, 'she is a millionairess in her own right.' I exploded. 'That puts the kibosh on your fantasies for a start. I'm a mere pauper!'

All the same, I went to dinner that night. At our second meeting I found Susan gay, amusing and good company. But right from the start it was Susan who made the running. As for marriage? Well, I was scared by the very thought. This time the lady was not too young, but too rich. Money seemed as great, if not a greater, barrier.

But there were other disparities between us. On that second night I was taken aback by the décor of the flat. There was gold paint everywhere and in the bathroom there were pure gold taps shaped like dolphins. I could imagine no place for my paintings among all that gold and chromium.

Despite such doubts, I had to admit to an increasingly strong physical attraction. On our frequent outings Susan introduced me as 'the famous film star', which made me writhe with embarrassment. When I demured, Susan retorted 'That description will soon be true again.' I had come to rely more and more on her judgement and opinions. When she said bluntly that my role as an agent did not suit me, I had to agree with her. But when she suggested that I could resume my film career if only I regained my confidence I could not go along with her, though for a moment I did consider trying to make a come-back.

In short, Susan took over the role of boss in my life. In my relations with women I have always been drawn to a dominant partner. Both Kay and Liz, in very different ways, were managerial types. I guess it shows a weak streak in my character, but I have always needed someone to lean on, someone to support my self-confidence.

To say that Susan bossed me into marriage is perhaps putting it a bit strongly. But when I protested that the financial gap between us was too great, she laughed and said 'Money is no barrier so far as I'm concerned. What's mine is yours.'

It was gentle, then tough persuasion from Liz and Mike that finally tipped the scales. They too dismissed the money barrier. 'Susan's not the type to rub your nose in her money bags,' scoffed Mike Todd. 'She's not a man-eater like Barbara Hutton.' Liz had the last word. 'You were never meant to be alone,' she argued. 'You need someone to share your life with. You know that?' I nodded silently. 'Well then,' she cried, 'here's a beautiful, warm-hearted woman whom you admit you fancy more than a bit?' I nodded again. 'Well,' cried Liz impatiently, 'what are you waiting for?'

My father, obviously somewhat over-awed by the powerful personality of my bride, attended the wedding. The night before he had said 'Are you sure you're doing the right thing, Mike? Not just marrying on the rebound?' I vehemently denied any such thing, but in retrospect I admit there was an element of rebound inasmuch as Susan's unquestioning faith in me helped heal my wounded ego. But at the start of our honeymoon money reared its ugly head. We plumped for a trip round the world and to pay my whack I was forced to sell a couple of paintings.

Back in England, I discovered that Susan fancied herself as an astute businesswoman and she now had a new financial ant in her pants. We had gone to live in Brighton for the summer, where Susan had a luxurious flat on the front. We had barely settled in when one day at breakfast she announced her intention of buying a restaurant in the Lanes. She took me along to inspect the premises, which had three floors, all badly in need of repair and decoration. 'Guess what I am going to call it?' she smiled. 'The Deserted Inn?' I suggested. Susan did not like the joke and said that this was a serious business proposition. 'Very well,' I said, 'seriously, what are you going to call it?' 'The Three Little Wilding Rooms,' she replied.

I was horrified. I told her that my name would no longer attract a sardine. But she was not to be thwarted. And further horror was to follow. She had decided to install me as a kind of maître d'hotel, which proved to be even worse miscasting than I had suffered in Hollywood. A maître d'hotel is supposed to remember people's names by way of flattering the customers. I have never been any good at remembering names. I was also supposed to recommend the speciality of the day and thus bump up the profits. I am no gourmet and I have no instant rapport with strangers. The whole ghastly thing not only embarrassed me, worse still it bored me and inwardly I was profoundly grateful when eventually the place closed.

Gradually Susan realised that in acquiring me as a husband she had acquired a phantom that only existed in her imagination. Our interests and characters really were incompatible and as the months went by we found we were having almost daily rows – which much to my regret soon became public property.

Our quarrels heralded the beginning of the end of our marriage. It died a sudden death when for once I made a decision. We were still living in Brighton, with my father a bewildered witness of our daily battles. I had flatly refused to accompany Susan to a party and, furious, she said she would go anyway. As soon as I heard the door close behind her, I rushed up to my father's room, where I found him deep in the *Times* crossword. I snatched the paper from his hands and shouted 'Pack your pyjamas and a toothbrush. I'm leaving this madhouse – and you're going with me.' My father did not show any surprise but looked up at me and in a mild voice said 'You mean you are doing a moonlight flit?' 'Exactly,' I replied. He shook my hand. 'Congratulations,' he smiled, 'I can't think why you haven't done it sooner.'

Fifteen minutes later, like a pair of absconding schoolboys, with only the clothes we stood up in and two small overnight bags we climbed into my car and headed for London. Intuitively, perhaps, I had not given up the lease of my Mayfair flat and now it provided a much-needed bolt-hole.

Soon after, Susan announced that she was divorcing me on grounds of desertion. Much to my surprise, for I had long since ceased to think of myself as newsworthy, my flat was besieged with members of the fourth estate asking the usual questions, which I refused to answer. But, when questioned by the press, Susan replied: 'I shall never marry another actor. I will never again be the breadwinner. A woman shouldn't earn more than her husband. It robs him of his manhood.'

Well, our marriage had certainly not robbed me of my manhood, but it had robbed me of the taste for matrimony. I had tried it three times and failed. In each case, I had to admit my own quota of blame. That was lesson enough for me.

The morning after our divorce became final, I received a call from Jerry Hogan. One of his most important clients wanted to return to England and her stage career, while he believed she had a great future in Hollywood . 'You can charm a monkey down from a tree,' he said, 'and that's what's needed. She isn't interested in money. Only sweet persuasion will make her return to Hollywood. Take the next plane out to New York and see what you can do.'

I obeyed orders, but didn't solve Jerry's problems. Indeed, I did exactly the reverse, when I met the one woman who was to bring me lasting happiness. Her name was Margaret Leighton.

14
Maggie and Me

I DO not believe in love at first sight, simply because I have never experienced it. But love at second sight is another matter, for that is what happened to Maggie and me.

I flew to New York to see Maggie purely in the capacity of an agent to try to sort out her career. I had no great hope about the success of my mission, nor indeed any burning desire to renew our brief acquaintance. Yet from the moment I stepped into her apartment I felt a tingle of excitement and I also immediately felt at home. Her choice of decoration showed exquisite taste, with purple carpets which highlighted the period furniture and white walls decorated with some interesting modern paintings, plus a couple of French impressionists.

There in the centre of this delightful setting, her arms outstretched to greet me, stood Maggie. She was wearing a long black dress which clung to every line of her graceful figure and her bounteous blonde hair was piled on top of her head in a Grecian knot. I thought I had never seen anyone so totally beautiful. Then we started talking, or rather she started talking and made me laugh. I hadn't laughed for some time and something told me she hadn't either.

We went out to dine at the Starlight Room at the St Regis Hotel and talked until dawn, without my once having raised the question of business. I think we both knew on that very first night that we would marry. I know I did, or at least hoped she would marry me.

But next morning, in the cold light of day, I dismissed the idea as pure fantasy. Why on earth should such a dazzling creature at the peak of her career even consider a 'has-been' like me as a husband? We met almost every night, and used to have long midnight conversations on the phone. The truth was that we had recognised each other's loneliness and there is nowhere in the world where you can feel quite so lonely as in the heart of Manhattan. Four weeks sped by and I hadn't even so much as touched her hand.

On New Year's Eve Maggie cooked us a delicious dinner. Around eleven o'clock we switched on the television and were watching the crowds congregating in Times Square, when suddenly Maggie suggested 'Why don't we go out and join them?' There was not a free taxi in sight, so we decided to brave the jostling crowds and walk. On the way we passed the Rockefeller Centre, the greatest precipice of light in the world. 'How about seeing the new year in from the top?' I suggested. 'All right,' she replied, 'I'm game. But only if you promise to hold my hand.'

The roof-top was crowded with revellers. We pushed our way to railings at the front. Below us stretched a vast vista of lights and towers. We stood silently for a moment, overwhelmed by the view, then I felt Maggie reach for my hand. 'You promised,' she whispered. Then suddenly we heard the first chime of midnight from St Patrick's Cathedral, followed by a chorus of sirens which seemed to come from every corner of the city. We found ourselves clasping hands with perfect strangers and joining in singing 'Auld Lang Syne' and I heard myself saying 'Since everyone else seems to be doing it, would you have any objection if I kissed you?' 'No objection at all,' replied Maggie and lifted her face to mine.

After the kiss, we drew away from each other overwhelmed by emotion. It was Maggie who found her

56 With Maggie on the set of *The Go-Between*, the last film she made

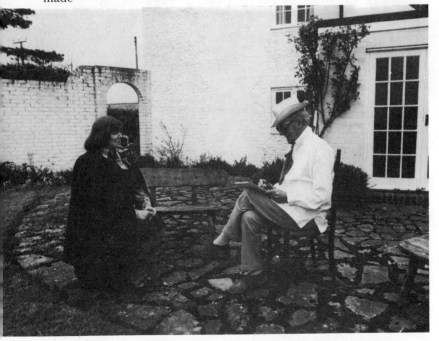

57 Sketching June, my faithful secretary and Girl Friday, at Gauntlet Cottage

58   Me at sixty-five

voice first. 'That must have been the tallest kiss in New York,' she said in a shaky little voice. I thought 'It's now or never' and replied 'Yes, and I must have the highest cheek of any man in the world to ask you this question. Don't hesitate to tell me if I embarrass you, but will you marry me?'

Maggie replied joyfully 'I'm not a bit embarrassed. But I would have been if you'd waited much longer, because I would have had to pop the question myself!'

If our courtship was unnecessarily drawn out because of my reticence, our wedding was to be subject to the law's interminable delay. Meanwhile, Jerry Hogan had won his battle over Maggie's future inasmuch as she agreed at least to give Hollywood a try. But neither of us relished the idea of starting our married life there. For me the very name of the place still tasted bitter on my tongue and Maggie had no airy-fairy dreams about overnight success. As we got off the plane at Burbank airport, she said 'I wish we had bought return tickets. Something tells me we are going to need them.'

Our arrival was conspicuous for the lack of press ballyhoo and we wanted to keep it that way. We installed ourselves in a modest but delightful house overlooking Pacific Palisades and Maggie soon transformed the interior into something that looked and felt like home. She asked me to cable my father to say we wanted him to be at the wedding. He was approaching eighty and now walked with sticks. He welcomed Maggie with open arms and on the evening of his arrival he said to me 'It looks as if you've found a woman to love you for youself at last, old chap. Mind you cherish her.'

All that remained was to find someone willing to marry us. Maggie had previously been married to Max Reinhardt and Laurence Harvey and in that city renowned for its marital break-ups we could not find a Justice of the Peace broadminded enough to marry a twice-divorced woman and a thrice-divorced man. Finally, after I had softened up the fourth JP on our list with a hundred-dollar bill, we were married in his living-room with his three noisy children playing at our feet.

We had done everything we could to keep our marriage a secret, but I think our JP must have picked up another hundred dollars by tipping off the press, for on the first morning of our honeymoon, which we had planned to spend quietly at our beach home, we awoke to find a gaggle of pressmen keeping vigil at our front door. Maggie was as horrified as I was and we dispatched my father to announce that we had gone away on our honeymoon, destination unknown.

By midday, when the coast seemed clear, we ventured outside and climbed into our car to buy groceries. But we had not reckoned on two dogged newsmen who jumped out of the bushes and blocked our driveway. They started on me first. 'What does Liz Taylor think of your remarriage?' they demanded. To which I replied that I didn't know and I didn't care. Then they attacked Maggie. 'What do you feel about your former husband's marriage to Harry Cohen's widow?' Maggie's reply was to wind up the car window in his face. 'Drive on, Mike!' she cried, white-faced with anger. 'And run 'em down if you can!'

When we returned from our shopping expedition, all seemed quiet. But my father had some ominous news. Our number was ex-directory, but somehow Louella Parsons had got hold of it and was demanding an interview. 'Let's go away. Now, tonight,' Maggie pleaded. 'An excellent idea,' I agreed, 'but where shall we go?' 'I don't care, anywhere so long as we can get some peace and quiet!'

We chose the Redwoods, home of the giant redwood trees, tucked away in the mountains just north of San Francisco, which offered primitive but cosy cabins and was an ideal hideaway. We threw some clothes into a bag and I took the wheel of the car, a Silver Ghost, Maggie's wedding present to me. We arrived about dusk and the chief forester guided us deep into the woods to a delightful little cabin, just one room containing little else besides a cooker, a fridge and an enormous bed. After we had unpacked, we held hands in front of the blazing log fire and listened to records of Maggie's beloved Mozart. Presently, feeling hungry, we raided the ice-box, where we found a large steak which I cooked with a fork over the open fire.

It must have been around midnight. Maggie was snuggled down in that enormous bed, while I was mixing us a goodnight noggin, when suddenly the cabin door burst open and standing on the threshold were two men with stockings over their faces. One of them had a sawn-off shotgun in his hands which he pointed directly at me. 'Put your hands up!' he demanded. I put my hands up.

The man walked up to me, the gun still pointing at my middle. 'Don't make no trouble and you won't get any. Just do as you're told.' Then with a wave of the shotgun he motioned to the other man. 'See to the dame,' he said. The second man walked over to Maggie, still in bed. 'Get up. And make it snappy!' he ordered. Maggie, cool as a cucumber, gave him one of her sweetest smiles. 'Certainly,' she said, 'but first hand me my dressing-gown. I am not used to receiving visitors in the nude.' The second man, stunned by her calmness, obeyed.

'Okay,' said the man with the gun, addressing Maggie, 'that's enough of your perk. Where do you keep your jewels?' 'At home in Santa Monica,' said Maggie in the tone of one dealing with an unruly child. 'A likely story,' snarled the man with the gun. Then, turning to the second man, he said 'Search the place.' The second man pulled open all the drawers, rifled our suitcases, looked under the bed and even in the ice-box.

I thought it was about time I showed some sang-froid. 'Look here,' I said, addressing the man with the shotgun, 'you've called at the wrong house. We're not millionaires.' The second man grunted 'That buggy parked outside. That don't belong to any cotton-pickers. Where's your dough?' 'What little I have with me is in my wallet on the dressing-table,' I replied. 'Take it with my compliments, then kindly leave us in peace.' The second man picked up the wallet and riffled through it. 'A lousy five hundred bucks!' he snarled. 'Guess we picked a duff couple.' 'Hold it,' said the man with the gun, and still keeping it trained on me, he strode over to Maggie. 'Hand over them sparklers,' he demanded, looking at the two rings Maggie was wearing. A ruby and diamond engagement ring and her wedding ring, a circlet of sapphires and diamonds.

'Here's my engagement ring,' said Maggie. 'It's worth $20,000. But please don't take my wedding ring. You see, we've just been married and it means so much to me.' Maggie's composure broke and there were tears running down her cheeks. The first man grunted. 'Okay, Ma'am. You win. Happens I'm a newly-wed myself. I reckon my gal would rather have her mitts cut off than part with the sparkler I gave her.' 'What's the matter with ya?' demanded the second man. 'Marriage turned you into a softie?'

'It's me that gives the orders round here,' said the man with the gun. 'Just you cut them telephone wires. Then let's get the hell out of here.' Growling like an angry bear, the second man pulled a knife from his pocket and did as he was told. As they went out of the door, the man with the gun lifted his hat in Maggie's direction. 'Good luck, Ma'am. Sorry if we interrupted your wedding night.' And the next moment the door closed behind them.

Maggie collapsed in my arms. I thought she was shaking with fright, but she was laughing through her tears as she kissed her wedding ring. 'The gangster with a heart of gold,' she exclaimed. 'It's straight out of a movie!'

But that was not, alas, the end of our honeymoon tribulations. The next morning, while Maggie was cooking bacon and eggs and I was still shaving, there was a hammering on our front door. Our early morning callers were two members of the state police. 'Sorry to disturb you, Mister,' said one of them, 'but were you disturbed by any intruders last night?' Of course, I told them the whole story. 'Count yourselves lucky,' responded the cop, 'you weren't the only victims. We've been besieged by phone calls since daybreak. Twenty other cabins were broken into and ransacked. Reckon they've made a killing.'

Then he wanted my name and address in case Maggie's ring was recovered. Like a fool I gave it to him. When we switched on the radio for the midday news, 'The Redwood Robbers' made the top news story of the day and to our dismay we were named as the chief victims. Two hours later the press, television and radio descended on us in force. Maggie, who had been so calm during the incident, threw a fit of hysterics and refused to let me open the door. 'Let them stay there,' she cried, 'I'm not going to be grilled by those vultures!' But come nightfall the persistent news seekers were still parked outside our front door. Finally I said to Maggie 'Look, they won't go away without some kind of statement. You stay here and I'll go out and see the buggers off.' It took Maggie twenty-four hours to calm down, but for the rest of our honeymoon the only encounters we had were with chipmunks and squirrels.

After our honeymoon we became involved in another incident, not so frightening but equally bizarre. We were at a first night at Grauman's Chinese cinema, where the stars leave their footprints in the cement. Hollywood may be crumbling, but a first night at Grauman's is still the signal for floodlights pointing into the sky and a throng of excited fans waiting for a glimpse of a star.

We were making our way slowly in the wake of stars pausing to sign autograph books when suddenly a blonde girl flung herself in front of us and threw her arms round Maggie's neck. The girl explained that she was a member of a local women's club who were planning a gala night to raise funds for cancer research – and would Maggie consider coming along as guest speaker? 'Please, please do say yes,' begged the girl. 'Your presence would guarantee a good turn-out and all in such a good cause.' I think it was this last plea that touched Maggie's heart. But when we got home that night she had second thoughts. 'I've never made a public speech before,' she said, 'and anyway, I don't see that my name is much of a draw in this neck of the woods. I doubt if I'll hear any more about it.' Nevertheless, two days later a formal invitation arrived. The notepaper was headed THE GREEN CARNATION CLUB. It had a downtown Los Angeles address, so we were not expecting Ciro's. All the same, I could not help a slight feeling of unease when we arrived at what looked like the entrance to a sleazy night-club.

We entered a musty-smelling hallway, with such dim lighting that at first I did not recognise the blonde girl we had met outside Grauman's. But there was no mistaking the nature of the other figure standing beside her. She was unashamedly butch. Her hair was Eton-cropped and she was dressed in white tie and tails complete with an artificial green carnation in her button hole.

'Allow me to introduce our president,' the blonde burbled proudly. Maggie stretched out her hand in greeting. Instead of shaking it in the conventional manner, the president bowed low and kissed it. Maggie didn't blink an eyelid, but followed our hostess through a curtain which led into a brilliantly lit room crammed to bursting with rows of chairs on which sat the strangest looking audience I had ever set eyes on. They were all female, but ninety per cent were dressed in masculine clothes, all sporting green carnations, which in some cases matched the colour of their hair. I even spotted one trousered female who gazed at the world through a monocle and another was puffing away at a cigar.

Acting on the spur of the moment, I said to the president 'Will you excuse my wife for a moment? She wants to go to the powder room.' And before she could protest, I dragged Maggie back through the curtains. 'Do you realise this club is made up of a bunch of lesbians?' I gasped. 'So what?' said Maggie, completely calm. 'Well,' I protested, 'supposing the press gets to hear about it?' 'Bugger the press,' replied Maggie. 'Anyway, you're a fine one to act prudish. Aren't some of your best friends gay?' 'But it's different for men,' I protested. Maggie let me have it between the eyes. 'I am here to raise funds for cancer victims,' she blazed. 'I don't suppose they would care what the sexual nature of their audience might be – providing it's a generous one.'

There was no answer to that. Maggie gave a brilliant talk and they proved a wonderful audience, sympathetic, attentive, and greeting Maggie's witticisms with appreciative laughter. At the end they gave her a standing ovation – in which I joined, feeling thoroughly ashamed of myself. The president set the appeal rolling and asked for those willing to donate a hundred dollars to raise their hands, but before the audience could react a melodious, slightly accented voice came from the back of the room: 'Please, Madam Chairman, will you start off by accepting my pledge of a thousand dollars?' Every head turned to see who the speaker was. And my eyes nearly popped out of my head. Dressed in a sparkling sequined gown, with white furs draped over her shoulders, stood one of the most erotic stars in Hollywood and certainly one of its greatest beauties.

We had been in Hollywood two months now and so far there was no sign of the golden future Jerry had predicted for Maggie. But we were still too deep in the throes of discovering new delights in one another's company to brood upon the unpredictability of Hollywood. Just the same, I sensed a growing restlessness in Maggie. Unlike me, Maggie was never completely happy unless she was working.

When her opportunity finally came it appealed both to us and to Jerry. She was invited to co-star opposite one of her favourite stars, Clark Gable. The story was set in an ex-servicemen's hospital for those disabled in the Second World War. Gable's role was that of a former man of action now confined to a wheelchair who has given up the will to live, until a nurse, played by Maggie, persuades, wheedles, and finally bullies him into resuming his place in the world. They fall in love, she overcomes his protestations, and eventually convinces him that they can live a full life together. The script was beautifully and sensitively written, the cameraman was Hollywood's best, James Wong Howe; and William Wyler was director. Maggie was so excited about the film that from the day she received the script she began to learn her lines, with me reading Gable's part.

Then the blow fell. One morning Jerry asked if he could come round to talk to Maggie about a new development. Maggie and I immediately sensed that he was the bearer of bad tidings. Maggie, who always came straight to the point, said jovially 'What's the matter, Jerry? Have they decided to cast Marilyn Monroe instead of me?' 'No, they still want you, but on certain conditions that are not going to make you very happy.'

Apparently, before finally making up his mind about casting Maggie in the part, Jack Warner wanted her to undergo a screen test. Maggie went up in smoke. 'Who does he think I am,' she exploded, 'a Warner starlet? If he wants proof of my ability as a screen actress, why doesn't he run *Under Capricorn*?' 'He's already done that,' replied Jerry, 'but he still insists on a screen test.'

Maggie seldom lost her temper, but when she did the results were volcanic. She began striding up and down the room venting her indignation in glacial tones. 'I haven't been asked to do an audition for the theatre since I became a star at the Old Vic at the age of twenty-one. As for screen tests, I've worked for Anthony Asquith, Carol Reed and Alfred Hitchcock, beside whom Jack Warner is just a junkyard creep. Did they ask me to do a screen test? No, they don't go in for insulting actresses or actors who have proved their worth.'

Poor Jerry, although visibly cringing under her attack, ventured to say 'I don't think Warner meant it as an insult. Why don't you take some time to think about it?' Maggie yelled 'There's nothing to think about! My mind is made up.' 'What shall I tell Warner?' asked Jerry. 'Tell him', said Maggie icily, 'that as far as a screen test is concerned, my answer is not fucking well likely!'

Now to those outside the profession Maggie's attitude may sound a bit high-handed. But several years later Wilfrid Hyde White took the same line when asked to do a screen test before being cast opposite Rex Harrison in *My Fair Lady*. Wilfrid's reaction, unlike Maggie's, was couched in impeccable English. 'If you apply the same rule to Rex Harrison,' he replied, 'I will be delighted to comply. Otherwise, look elsewhere.' Wilfrid won the day. He got the role without a test. Alas, not so poor Maggie. Jerry tried in vain to reach a compromise, but it was a case of the immovable sensitivity of an actress.

Unlike myself, who had clung to the hope of a Hollywood career and accepted roles which insulted my good sense, Maggie was perceptive enough to see that Hollywood offered her no acceptable future. She described to me her feelings about Hollywood by quoting an author who said of his old school that he liked everything about it except 'the lessons, the masters, the boys and the games'.

Shortly after the Warner fiasco, she turned to me and said 'Oh, darling, I cannot live in this place any longer. Apart from the people, I hate a place where there are no seasons. I feel as if I have stopped growing. I'm sure God made Hollywood for humming-birds. They only live one year. Wise God, wise birds. Let us get out now before we both become pallbearers to the humming-birds.'

Then, right out of the blue, a cable arrived which was the answer to Maggie's despair. It was an invitation from John Clements to join his Chichester Theatre Company for their 1969 season. To Maggie it was an offer to return to her first and truest love, the stage, and I was infected with her joy when she cabled acceptance.

Two weeks later we left Hollywood. 'Any regrets?' I asked Maggie as we boarded the plane. Her reply was to take my hand and say 'Only that we have wasted the first year of our married life in this God-forsaken city.'

Arriving at Chichester, we were touched by the fact that

John Clements and the whole company were waiting to give us a heart-warming welcome. For the first month we stayed at a hotel and on Sundays I used to drive Maggie round the beautiful Sussex countryside. It was on one such drive that we saw a cottage for sale with whitewashed walls and red gabled roof, nestling right in the heart of the Downs. From that first glance we felt we had found our ideal home. Next day I phoned the estate agent and made an appointment to view it. The interior proved as dream-like as the exterior – spacious rooms with bay windows overlooking the Downs, three delightful bedrooms and, to Maggie's delight, a very well equipped modern kitchen. The cottage was remote from even the nearest village and I asked Maggie if she would not feel too isolated. 'Oh, no!' she replied, 'isolation with you would be my idea of Heaven!' We decided to buy it there and then, and through the twelve years of our married life we never regretted our decision.

Marriage, no matter how much you may be in love, always proves a voyage of discovery. One thing I was soon to learn about my fourth wife was her deep concern for the well-being of her fellow artists. If any were ever in trouble or in need of sympathy or advice, Maggie was the first person they would turn to.

One example was Dame Sybil Thorndike. If Maggie could not be present at one of her first nights, even if it meant a transatlantic phone call, Dame Sybil would call Maggie – a practice that had begun over twenty-five years before, when they first met at the Old Vic. Dame Sybil once told me: 'Talking to Maggie is the best tonic I know for first night nerves.'

Vivien Leigh would pour out her heart to Maggie, particularly during the last months of her tragically short life when she was suffering from increasingly deep depressions. Often our phone would ring in the early hours of the morning and, since Maggie was working in the theatre and Vivien's calls were becoming more and more frequent, I once suggested that we leave the receiver off the hook. Maggie replied reproachfully 'Would you refuse a lifebelt to a drowning woman?'

Maggie also had a strong mothering instinct. This was never more in evidence than in her relationship with the actor Robert Newton. An incurable alcoholic, during the last years of his life he was increasingly shunned as a social outcast. His fellow actors gave a cruel twist to the saying 'drunk as a newt' by coining the phrase 'drunk as a Newton'. But if ever they displayed such unkindess in Maggie's presence she would turn on them in fury, saying 'Bob is a great actor. The fact that he also has the misfortune to be an alcoholic is not a joke, it's a tragedy.'

In the next ten years I made only two screen appearances, a small role in *Waterloo* and an even smaller role in *Lady Caroline Lamb*. Both occurred early in our marriage, and only because Maggie persuaded first the producers and then me. She felt I was taking the easy way out by not pursuing my career on either stage or film. But when she saw what the effort of appearing before the camera was doing to me she gave up pushing and, though we never said as much in words, accepted that I had packed in my career.

By the end of our fifth year of marriage my whole life revolved around Maggie. I helped her learn her lines, gave advice on her costumes and, as a member of the audience, cried with joy over her many triumphs. At home, I ran the ship: kept accounts, did the shopping, the cooking and even the washing-up. Such a description makes it sound as if I took a secondary role in our lives together and that it was an unequal partnership. But Maggie never made me feel I was living in her shadow. It is true Maggie organised our lives, but she was much too clever to let me or anyone else know that she was doing it. For instance, she would say to visiting friends 'Michael said so-and-so', or 'Michael has decided', while all the time it was she who had made the decisions. She never treated me as anything but the kingpin of our marriage, yet in reality she was the dominant partner – and I guess that's what I had been searching for all my life.

The reasons for my adoration of Maggie would be self-evident to anyone who ever knew her. But what about her reasons for loving me? Well, to anyone who has ever known me that will remain a mystery. But an incident occurred during our fourth year of marriage which reveals the depths of Maggie's feelings. The *Sunday Times* had organised an exhibition at the Round House entitled 'Cinema City', which brilliantly re-created the history of the cinema. The main part of the day's programme was a re-showing of Anna's, Herbert's and my own most successful films. Afterwards, the manager had arranged for the three of us to appear on the stage and answer questions from the audience. Despite the comforting presence of both George Perry, who unlike most chairmen knew what he was talking about, and Maggie in the audience, I went on stage half stifled with my usual dose of nerves and sat in my chair with as much animation as a scarecrow. Anna and Herbert were their usual entertaining selves, but questions directed at me were slow in coming and I was even slower in answering them and gradually sank lower and lower into my chair, feeling like an oaf.

Sensing my misery, Maggie rose to her feet and said in a clear ringing voice 'Ask my husband how he learned to dance for *The Glass Slipper.*' Adroitly, George Perry said, 'I think the questioner is the famous actress, Margaret Leighton. Am I right?' This brought a storm of applause and I thought to myself, well at least the audience likes my wife. And her question had given me the chance I had been waiting for. I started to explain my agonising experiences with my jockstrap while I was learning to dance ballet and I knew I was off the hook. The audience were laughing with me, not at me. From that point on they seemed to think everything I said was funny.

After the laughter had died down and I stepped forward to receive the applause, Maggie clutched at a friend's arm and, her eyes brimming with tears, said 'Oh, I'm so glad I was the last to get him!' 'You make it sound as if you did the proposing!' remarked our friend. Laughing through her tears, Maggie replied 'No. I may have led him to the brink if you can call the top of the Rockefeller Building the brink, but it was Mike who did the proposing and now we are married it's Mike who does the disposing. At least that's what he thinks. And that's how it should be – and by God I'm going to keep it that way!'

But Maggie, for all her understanding nature, could not control a feeling natural in any woman, a jealousy of my past which blew up one day into the nearest we ever came to a row. It happened when she was sorting out my collection of photographs. It took her two days and from time to time she would show me a photo and ask me to confirm the date or occasion. Among the photos were quite a number taken with film stars, signed in most intimate terms. I noticed her getting more quiet and withdrawn until the second evening, when she announced at about seven o'clock that I could get my own supper for once and she was going to bed.

Thick-skulled ass that I am, I did not realise what was wrong until I had made myself a cold supper, watched the night's sports news and finally gone upstairs to bed myself. To my surprise the bed was empty. I knocked on the bathroom door and when there was no reply, opened it. No sign of Maggie. Alarmed, I went into the passage and called her name. Then I heard the muffled sound of sobbing coming from the spare room. I knocked and heard her tearful voice saying 'Go to hell!'

A minute later, I was holding her in my arms. 'Mag,' I pleaded, desperately puzzled, 'what on earth's the matter?' 'Those photos,' she sobbed, 'I wanted to burn the lot!' 'But why?' I asked. She sat up and, pounding me on the chest, yelled 'Because I'm jealous. Do you understand, you numbskull? I'm plain jealous and God-damned ashamed of it!'

I tried to explain that those photos represented my past.

I was not jealous of her past. Why should she be jealous of mine? She flashed back with fury 'Because your past represents a regiment of women! I bet every time you kiss me, you compare me with Dietrich or Taylor.' I replied quietly 'You're right. When we were first married I sometimes made comparisons. Not often, but sometimes. And you know what my answer always was? I said to myself I have only one regret in life and that is that you were not my first as well as my last love.'

To complete our household, through my old friend and neighbour Michael Trubshawe, we were lucky enough to find a gem of a girl in June Peskett, who acted as Maggie's secretary and as general housekeeper. June had three children – the eldest, Tim; a charming teenage daughter, Melody; and six-year-old Kelly, to whom Maggie immediately became so attached that she played the role of an adopted aunt, buying his clothes, helping him with his homework, playing toy soldiers with him on the dining-room table.

Those first ten years of our marriage were the happiest and best years of my life. Never before had I found another human being with whom I was so completely in tune. There was a sort of magical telepathy between us. We each knew what the other was thinking without the need for words.

During those years, Maggie's reputation was growing with each succeeding season, whereas my name was receding with the memories of the fifties. Yet in public or in the company of friends she always seemed to have the knack of turning the spotlight on me. We also found we had the capacity to make each other laugh. Maggie was one of the wittiest women I have ever known, yet when we had company she would always take a back seat and urge me to tell an anecdote or joke, despite the fact that she might have heard it a dozen times before. She revelled in showing me off to my best advantage, wanting others to see me through her eyes. It was like being born again.

Perhaps I can best convey the secret of our relationship by recalling a remark made by John Clements. He was just leaving our cottage after a very happy reunion when he put his arms round us both and said 'You know, seeing you two together reminds me of two battered ships who have sailed through stormy seas but have at last come safely home to harbour.'

15
Tragedy

'I WAS only ten at the time, but I'll always remember a sad story our English mistress read to us. It told of a man who searched the world for what he called his "other half". He believed that human beings are all born separate halves of a whole and we are all incomplete until we find our true loves. Well, he finally found his other half, only to have her die in his arms. Darling Mike, I feel that you and I are two parts of a whole. Aren't we lucky to have found ourselves in life?'

Maggie told me this story on our wedding anniversary, sitting in our garden while I was drawing her portrait. When it was finished, she took one look at it and exclaimed 'Why have you made my eyes so sad?'

I did not know it at the time, but Maggie was already beginning to suffer from the pains that were to develop into her fatal illness. Today every time I look at that portrait, which stands on my mantelpiece, I see what she meant. The sadness reflects more than the pain she was suffering; it is as if she was gazing beyond me, beyond life itself into the unknown – and I often wonder if that look in her eyes came from a presentiment of her own death.

The first sign of her illness was when she bent down to pick up a newspaper from the floor and remained bent like a corkscrew, unable to straighten up without help. At the time she laughed it off as 'pangs of old age', but I began to notice that she had increasing difficulty in going up and down stairs. When I went to help her, she brushed me aside angrily, saying 'Don't treat me like an invalid!'

Then one day she fell down trying to get into the car. This time I was adamant about seeing a doctor. I was with her as she described her symptoms. The doctor seemed infuriatingly unconcerned and appeared to agree with Maggie's diagnosis. He made out a prescription for pain-killing tablets and told her to come back in a month's time if her condition had not improved.

But Maggie's health did not improve. As the weeks went by she could no longer hide her frequent pain, though the bottle of pain-killers stood still unopened on her dressing-table and she stubbornly refused to visit the doctor again.

It was agonising watching the person I loved most in the world suffering increasing pain, yet refusing all help and advice. Her attacks became part of our daily lives. When we were sitting watching television, suddenly beads of perspiration would break out on her forehead and her face would contract with pain. She would lightly make some excuse to go to bed early and I would sit there listening to her stumbling up the stairs like an old woman.

One night I could bear it no longer. I followed her up to our bedroom, picked up the bottle of pills and urged her to take one. 'They can't do any harm,' I said, 'and I can no longer bear to see you suffering unnecessary pain.' Maggie grimaced, but for once gave in and did as I asked her.

After that for a month she appeared to be free from pain. But I could not help noticing that the bottle of pain-killers quickly dwindled. Then, as if beaten in a game, she asked me to phone the doctor for a new prescription. 'I suppose those beastly pills are the lesser of two evils,' she admitted, 'but God save me from ever becoming dependent on them.'

The challenge came when John Clements offered her the leading role in his Chichester Theatre production of *Reunion in Vienna*. She accepted without a second thought, saying 'I'm not going to let a few aches and pains stand in the way of my career.'

I went along to rehearsals and, although she would be all right in the mornings, at the end of the day there was no disguising her decided limp. But when John and I expressed concern she assured us both that she would be fine on the opening night. 'There's no doctor as good as Dr Footlights,' she assured us gaily, and John took her at her word and, like her fellow actors, turned a blind eye to her obvious disability.

The day of the first performance started disastrously. Maggie had one of her worst attacks yet, so bad that by five o'clock she was unable to get out of bed. 'You can't possibly go on tonight,' I said. 'I'm going to phone John and tell him so.' She snatched the phone from my hands, white with rage. 'You'll do no such thing!' she blazed, 'I haven't missed a first night in thirty years. And I'm not missing this one. Just help me get dressed and drive me to the theatre.'

I sat with her in her dressing-room as with shaking hands she applied her make-up and her dresser helped her struggle into her costume. Then came the familiar back-stage call, 'Overture and beginners. Ten minutes, please.' The call acted like an electric shock. Bracing every nerve of her body, Maggie got to her feet and stood erect for the first time that day. 'You see,' she cried, 'I can do it.' I produced the bottle of pills from my pocket. 'These might help,' I suggested. Maggie shook her head. 'No,' she replied, 'It's a case of mind over matter. Go, darling, please go now and don't come back until the performance is over.'

Sick with apprehension, I took my seat in the stalls. The curtain went up and five minutes later Maggie made her entrance. I could have leapt to my feet and cheered. She strode onto the stage with the confidence of an Amazon and stood smiling and steady as a rock as she was greeted by loud applause. Throughout the next two and a half hours, during which Maggie was hardly off stage for more than a couple of minutes, she never wavered in her movements or fluffed a line.

As the curtain fell, I rushed backstage to her dressing-room door. I entered to find her bent over her dressing-table in a state of total collapse, but undaunted she grinned at me like a triumphant schoolgirl. 'I told you Dr Footlights would see me through,' she cried.

But offstage Dr Footlights could not help her. Gardening had always been Maggie's favourite hobby, but she was forced to give it up when one day I found her collapsed on a flower-bed with blood flowing from her head, where she had fallen on the edge of a spade. She had also always enjoyed cooking, but a string of accidents eventually forced her tacitly to hand over the kitchen to June Peskett. Nor could she any longer play hide-and-seek with Kelly, and her hands were so shaky that she could not even happily help him play with his toy soldiers.

Maggie now spent most of the day in bed or lying on a couch in the living-room. All her life she had been an avid reader of poetry and prose, but she would pick up a book then put it down, as if the effort of concentration was too great, and she no longer took any interest in the newspapers or television. Only two things remained – her natural gaiety and her dedication to the theatre. As the Chichester season wore on somehow, miraculously, Maggie played three leading roles without a break, but it was now obvious that even Dr Footlights could no longer sustain her.

As it happened, the final shattering diagnosis came not as a result of a visit to a doctor but at the end-of-season party. I had guided Maggie, who leaned on my arm for much-needed support, across the stage where the party was being held and sat her down in an easy chair, when a total stranger came up to us and said 'Excuse me, Mr Wilding, could I have a private word with you?' He explained that he was an old friend of Sir Ralph Richardson's and had recently retired to live in Chichester. He did not mention the nature of his former profession or I might have been at least a little prepared for the shock to come.

He led me to a quiet corner of the stage and without more ado, came straight to the point. 'I am sorry to have to tell you, Mr Wilding, that your wife is suffering from multiple sclerosis.'

I was completely stunned. 'How can you form such a diagnosis by watching my wife walk across the stage?' I demanded. 'I have spent a lifetime studying nervous diseases,' he replied quietly, 'and I advise an immediate visit to my former partner who is also an expert in this field of medicine.' Then he handed me a card bearing a Harley Street address.

The next morning I felt utterly dazed. At first I told myself that surely such an off-the-cuff diagnosis could not be accurate. Then I took down my father's medical dictionary and looked up the details of the disease, about which I knew little or nothing. With sinking heart, I found the description of the symptoms tallied too closely with Maggie's for me to dismiss the idea out of hand, appalling as it seemed. My next thought was 'How do I get Maggie to see that specialist without mentioning those two dreaded words?' In the end I rang up Michael Trubshawe and as usual he came up with a practical solution. Maggie had promised me she would see a doctor on the supposition that she was suffering from severe rheumatism and it was under this pretext that I finally persuaded her to see a specialist.

Maggie asked me to accompany her into the consulting-room. After a thorough examination the specialist confirmed my worst fears. 'Mrs Wilding,' he said, 'you strike me as a woman of courage. I don't think you would appreciate me beating about the bush. I am sorry to have to tell you but you are suffering from a nervous disease known as multiple sclerosis.' Maggie looked at him calmly and in the most matter of fact voice said 'That's something people die of, isn't it?' 'Not invariably,' the specialist assured her gently. 'You are still a young woman, which is important.' 'What's important,' retorted Maggie, 'is whether my condition is curable.' The specialist replied that he could not offer hope of a complete cure, but could prescribe a course of drugs to control the condition and alleviate the pain.

I was too horrified to find words. I could not then and never did face up to the possibility of Maggie's eventual death. But I think she did, although during the last two years of her life she only once again put the possibility into words. It happened when some friends of ours had come over to the cottage for tea. By this time Maggie's hands were badly affected and I could see our friends trying not to notice her difficulty in raising her cup to her lips. Suddenly, as casually as if she were talking about the weather, Maggie said 'You know, in a way, I'm glad I have this illness. It means I shall die before Mike.'

Maggie's courage was truly amazing. She never lost the will to live. For her, to live meant to act. Indeed, her last years were the years that brought her most acclaim. In 1972 she was awarded the CBE. The following year she received the award for the best supporting performance of the year in Joseph Losey's film *The Go-Between* and, as well as several successes on television, she stole the film *Lady Caroline Lamb*, with her smouldering portrait of the heartless Lady Melbourne. Then in 1974 Maggie was offered a choice of two plum stage roles. One was in the American hit *A Little Night Music*; the other, opposite Alec Guinness in Ivy Compton-Burnett's *A Fortune in the Family*.

But, however flattering these offers were, it was now apparent that her affliction was known in the world of the theatre if not to the public, for both roles called for a portrayal of a semi-invalid. As usual, Maggie made a joke of the implications. 'If I don't watch out,' she remarked to me with a laugh, 'I shall find myself type-cast.'

She settled for *A Fortune in the Family*, which she played in a wheelchair, and received some of the best notices of her career. The *Evening Standard* wrote: 'Maggie can hang up the pictures and lay down the carpet in her dressing-room. She is here to stay for a long run and there is no better performance in town.'

In fact it only ran for a year because of Guinness's previous commitments, but always to packed houses. During the run, I saw a television interview which made me writhe with fury. An insensitive interviewer asked Maggie 'Is there something special about you yourself being an invalid that helps you play this part so realistically?' To which Maggie retorted 'There is nothing special about me. Nor do I consider myself an invalid. I am what I have been all my life. Just an ordinary actress doing her best.'

Maggie's reply reveals her modesty. About that time she told me 'I would like to be remembered as an actress who always did her best. Sometimes I have succeeded, sometimes I have failed. But I have never given less than my best.' She was underrating herself to think that her best was ever less than brilliant. Indeed, after the last performance of the play John Gielgud visited her dressing-room and, as he leaned over to kiss her hand, he said 'As always, Maggie, you are never just good in a part. You are always perfect.'

At the end of the year's run we returned thankfully to the peace and quiet of the cottage. Although she would not admit it, after a year in which she had never missed a performance Maggie was so completely exhausted that for a week she did little more than sleep. But, alas, my hopes that a complete rest would improve her condition proved false. Without the nightly dose of adrenalin provided by the theatre, not only did her pains return with renewed ferocity but for the first time since I had known her she sank into fits of deep depression. When the specialist prescribed stronger drugs to combat the pain, she took them without a murmur and with the respite they provided began to regain a semblance of good spirits.

Nevertheless, Maggie's illness now took a turn for the worse. The drugs, although they dulled the pain, could not stem the awful attacks which shook her whole body and she had difficulty in breathing.

At first, when she felt these attacks coming on, she tried

to hide them from me by locking herself in the bedroom and when I begged her to let me in she would scream 'Go away. I want to be left alone. Go away!'

An hour, sometimes two, would pass and I would sit downstairs alone feeling completely helpless. Then the bedroom door would open and I could hear her stumbling footsteps on the stairs and she would make a sort of stage entrance, perfectly made-up, looking glamorous in her negligée, walk over and kiss me on the forehead, and say 'Count to ten and Maggie will be herself again!' And sure enough ten minutes later she would be restored to her old joke-cracking self or would challenge me to a game of chess.

Despite these moods of gaiety, she had by now accepted the fact that the time was not far off when she would become a complete invalid confined to a wheelchair. She never said as much, but one morning I found her deep in consultation with an architect about plans to build an extra ground-floor room specially designed to meet the needs of a disabled person.

Having dismissed the architect, she picked up the phone and called her agent with instructions that he was to start making plans for a new career in radio. 'I may not be able to totter up to Broadcasting House on my own pins any more,' she said, 'but I can make recordings from home and I would like to try my hand at something challenging. Ibsen, Conrad, Shaw . . . I feel like an actress who is just entering the best years of her career. The autumn years when one is mature. My limbs may have given up on me, but not my voice or my brain.'

Within a week offers came pouring in and Maggie sat up all night reading parts, asking for criticism, full of anticipation and excitement about the future.

But a month or so after she had been talking about the new room she was reading a part out loud to me when suddenly she bent double and screamed for me to bring her pills. She swallowed a handful, then after about twenty minutes the spasms stopped and she fell into a fitful sleep, only to wake up every half-hour or so crying with pain. I had never seen her cry before and was deeply alarmed and suggested calling the doctor. But she was her usual stubborn self and just asked for a sleeping pill. Finally, around six in the morning, she fell into a deep sleep.

Although I scarcely slept myself, nevertheless I woke around eight and crept out of the bedroom, leaving Maggie sleeping peacefully. It must have been about midday when I ventured upstairs and knocked on the bedroom door. 'Come in, darling!' she cried gaily. She was still in bed, but was on the telephone chatting away nineteen to the dozen to her agent. She paused, putting her hand over the mouthpiece, and said to me 'Bring me a cup of coffee, there's a love', and resumed her conversation.

Five minutes later I returned to the bedroom. The receiver was dangling from the hook and Maggie's whole body was writhing in terrible spasms, her breath rattling drily in her throat. I grabbed the phone and dialled the doctor. Mercifully, he answered and said 'I'll be there in ten minutes. In the meantime, call an ambulance.' After I had done that, I yelled for June, who came dashing up from the kitchen. Maggie's awful spasms had now ceased and she appeared to have lapsed into unconsciousness and she was still unconscious when the ambulance arrived at the hospital.

June and I sat in the waiting-room chain-smoking. An hour went by and I could stand it no longer. I buttonholed the first nurse to pass and demanded information. At that moment the doctor appeared with the specialist in charge of Maggie's case. He told me she was in a coma and there was no knowing when, if at all, she would recover consciousness. I begged him to let me sit at her bedside and he led me down the corridor to the room in which Maggie lay. My first thought was how peaceful she looked, like a child who had just fallen asleep. I pulled up a chair and sat by her side. Two – maybe three – hours went by, interrupted by regular visits from the specialist, who listened to her heartbeat and took her pulse.

It must have been about ten o'clock when June, who had been sitting by herself in the waiting-room, tiptoed into the room and made the whispered suggestion that I might let her take over for ten minutes, while I had a coffee and a cigarette. But I said 'No, I'm staying here in case she wakes up.' June returned a few minutes later with the specialist who argued that the coma might last indefinitely and, anyway, I could not go through the whole night without sleep. I replied 'I'm not leaving this building while there is still a chance my wife might need me.' The specialist said 'I know how you feel, but I've fixed up a bed for you just down the corridor in case you feel like sleeping.'

They had left the room only a few minutes when I noticed Maggie's eyelids fluttering. Suddenly she opened her eyes and gazed up at me, her face transformed by a smile. Her lips moved, but uttered no sound. Then, just as suddenly, her eyes closed and her head fell to one side on the pillow.

I dashed into the corridor, calling for help at the top of my voice. The next thing I knew, I was surrounded by nurses who assured me the specialist was on his way and firmly piloted me into the waiting-room. June was still there. We must have sat there for about half an hour, not exchanging a word, when the specialist appeared in the doorway. He walked straight up to me and put his arm round my shoulder, saying 'I'm sorry, but there was nothing anyone could do. I am afraid she has gone.'

The specialist led us back along the corridor without a word and opened the door of Maggie's room, saying to June 'I think you had better go in with him.' I knelt by Maggie's bed, took her hand, spoke her name over and over again. Then, still in a state of hysterical disbelief, I took my glasses off and held them to her lips to see if she was still breathing. June began to cry, then pulled herself together and led me gently out of the room.

When we got back to the cottage, I just sat there in my chair dumb and stunned. June called some good friends of ours who were near neighbours, and although it was past midnight they came round immediately and persuaded me to have a drink. I had one, then another and another and the stimulus of alcohol combined with shock summoned up in me the wild hope that there had been some terrible mistake. Despite their protestations I insisted on calling the hospital. I got through to Maggie's ward and asked if there was any change in her condition. I was answered by what seemed a cold and unfeeling voice, but which was only reporting the fact when it said 'Of course there is no change, Mr Wilding. Your wife is dead.'

The subsequent post-mortem showed the extent of Maggie's courage. The doctor who performed the autopsy reported that considering the grievous lesions found in her spinal cord it was incredible that she had stayed so long on her feet. Anyone with less courage would have been confined to a wheelchair long before.

My sensation of disbelief continued even to the day of the funeral. I noticed the details, the display of flowers and wreaths outside the church and the faces of the mourners. But I was too numb with grief to accept that I would never see Maggie again. The only moment of the ceremony which penetrated my numbness was when John Clements, who gave the funeral address, quoted words of Maggie's own choice, which she had once read aloud to me. They were Ellen Terry's dying words: 'I hope my friends and fellow artists will remember the happy times, the laughter. Forget the rest.'

After the ordeal of the service several close friends came back to the cottage. As I stood there listening to the expressions of sympathy and condolence, out of the corner of my eye I saw June's son Kelly standing by himself in a corner. I went over to him and asked 'Would you like a Coca-cola or lemonade?' He shook his head. 'Not thirsty,' he said. 'What about some potato crisps, then?' I suggested. 'Not hungry either,' he mumbled. Sensing he was on the edge of tears, I patted him on the shoulder. 'Poor us. We are both going to miss our Maggie, aren't we?' 'Yes,' he replied in a strangled voice. 'She was a good bloke.'

Although I had heard many moving tributes to Maggie that day, Kelly's gruff little remark moved me more than any. I could find no words to comfort him, nor could I bear the company of Maggie's mourners any longer. Without a word of farewell or thanks, I turned my back on the crowded room, shut the door and walked upstairs to our bedroom. Then I locked the door and sat down on the bed and wept.

16

Stage Fright

SINCE Maggie's death life has never been the same and since she died I have suffered increasingly from blackouts, an affliction which has dogged me since I was a teenager.

The first of these blackouts occurred when I was eighteen. I was in my mother's kitchen at the time and had just picked up a box of eggs – the next thing I knew I was lying under the table covered with eggshells. My mother thought it was a fainting fit and with the buoyancy of youth I dismissed the incident completely from my mind. Six years later, during my tour with Fay Compton in Australia, I learned the truth. I had gone to see a doctor because I was not feeling well and, after a brief examination, he said 'I'm afraid you've got epilepsy, old sport. Afraid there's no cure. It's something you'll have to learn to live with. There is, however, one thing you must do and that's keep off the spirits. Drink wine or beer.' Since in those days I could not afford wine and did not care for beer, for a while I must have been the most sober actor alive – good enough for the *Guinness Book of Records*.

In 1977 I revealed the nature of my illness for the first time in an interview with Tony Wilmot for the magazine *Weekend*. When his article appeared, I received literally hundreds of letters from those similarly afflicted, saying that I had helped them overcome the fears and embarrassments caused by epilepsy and that they had been encouraged by my example, for if despite my handicap I had made good in life then there was hope for them.

Now that I have reached old age, the malady has worsened and in recent years I have found myself falling about all over the place like a knockabout comic. Indeed, on one occasion I came to in a twisted heap at the foot of the stairs, without any recollection of how I got there. Another time I hit my head against a solid oak side-table with such force that the table broke in half.

This ailment was in fact partly responsible for my retirement from acting, though the reason for my premature retirement really goes back to 1952, when I made the fatal mistake of leaving Herbert for Hollywood. It would, however, be wrong simply to blame Hollywood. The truth is that my confidence in myself as an actor was never very strong; otherwise I would have recovered from the traumas of Hollywood, as many had done before me.

My stage fright dates back to the fifties too. When I had been twelve years away from the footlights, Noel Coward asked me to take over John Gielgud's role in his play *Nude with a Violin*. Naturally I was flattered and had every reason to be confident. When my name appeared on the billings advance bookings soared. Noel himself made the comment, 'You are an even bigger box-office draw than John.'

The first night went off well and reviewers compared me favourably with Gielgud. After a month playing to packed houses, I felt I had found my stage feet again. Then it happened. One night, about half an hour before curtain up, I felt one of my heads coming on. Noel had been paying one of his frequent visits to my dressing-room and I turned to him and said 'It's no good. My understudy will have to go on.' 'Not on your nelly!' retorted Coward. 'Please,' I begged him, 'I shall never live it down if I black out on stage.' Noel was adamant, saying 'You'll be all right once you're out front.' But I was far from all right. I don't recall a moment of that performance. I played it in a trance, able to see the other actors only as blurred figures and continually knocking into props. A lot of people thought I was drunk and walked out, and when I came on to take my call there was booing from the gallery. It was a terrifying experience.

However, even that is not the full reason for my premature retirement. The complete answer, I suspect, lies deep in my character. Peter Graves said to me many years ago 'Acting is seventy-five per cent charm and talent. Few have that extra driving force to get to the top and stay there. Call it twenty-five per cent devil.' You might say that I lacked that twenty-five per cent devil. Herbert described my fear of the stage even more dramatically when he wrote in his autobiography 'Whereas Anna loved acting, Michael hated it.' I wouldn't go that far. I think it would be nearer the mark to say not that I hated acting, but that I feared it. I was not a born actor and the art of acting never came to me easily.

So I would put down my premature retirement to the nightmare of Hollywood, my illness and my lack of self-confidence. And there is one other factor, the fact that I am basically lazy.

But, thanks to Maggie, I haven't entirely lazed away my old age. As soon as we settled in the cottage, she urged me to start painting again. She had seen the portraits I had done of Liz and my two sons and said 'You had a great gift which you've thrown away. Why not give it another chance?' Now that I am alone, between bouts in hospital, I have followed her advice and the results are not unpleasing. The doctor at the local hospital where I was recently a patient for a while even suggested that I should give art lessons to the patients as a kind of therapy.

Looking back on my life, I suppose it is natural to ask 'Do I have any regrets?' Well, that's a facer all right. Not working hard enough, I suppose. Not being kinder to people. There is always room for improvement in that department.

Recently an old friend who interviewed me asked me if,. like Hamlet, mine was the story of a man who could not make up his mind. It is, I fear, all too apt an analogy. The same interviewer asked me whether, considering my lack of self-confidence, my lack of ambition and the ever-present shadow of illness, was it not a miracle that I ever became an actor, let alone a star?

Without hesitation I patted him on the back and replied 'Well put!' Then, handing him his drink, I repeated, 'Well put, indeed!'

Epilogue
by Pamela Wilcox

O N the morning of Saturday 16 July 1979 June Peskett
was a little later than usual arriving at the cottage. As
she drove up to the front door, she was horrified to see
Michael Wilding standing on the doorstep waiting for her,
his face covered with blood. Gently she led him, shaking
from head to foot, into the drawing-room, sat him down in
an armchair and called the doctor. Then she set about trying
to wash away the blood which stuck in clots to his face and
in his hair. Although shaking from shock, Michael was
completely coherent, explaining that he had had another
of his blackouts and that when he came to he found he had
fallen against the fire-irons, which had split his skull
open.

When the doctor arrived, he took one long look at the
gaping head wound and told Michael he was calling an
ambulance at once to take him to hospital. June went with
him in the ambulance, while Michael, who had refused to
be carried on a stretcher or to lie down, sat swearing at the
medical profession in general and hospitals in particular.

June was sitting in the waiting-room when the doctor
finally reappeared. He reported that no internal damage
had shown up on the X-rays, but because of the severity of
the injury so close to the brain he was worried about the
possibility of a blood clot forming.

When June entered the room, Michael appeared to be
sleeping peacefully, so she sat down silently and tried to
concentrate on reading a magazine. It was about four
o'clock when Michael opened his eyes and said 'Oh God,
June, I feel bloody awful!' Then he lapsed into a coma.

June immediately alerted his two sons, who drove down from London and joined her in the vigil beside the bed. At about eleven o'clock that night the specialist, who had been making hourly visits, told them that there was no change in Michael's condition. He was still in a deep coma and likely to remain so indefinitely. The specialist added that there was really no point in prolonging their vigil and advised them to go home, saying that he would notify them immediately if there was any change.

At 4 a.m. the phone rang in the cottage. June, who had been dozing in a chair, picked up the receiver. It was the doctor, who asked to speak to Michael junior. 'I'm sorry to have to tell you some sad news, my boy,' said the doctor gently. 'Your father died peacefully in his sleep about half an hour ago.'

The next day the specialist reported that the autopsy had revealed a long-formed blood clot on the brain and so Michael had been spared lingering on like a cabbage. Later the specialist told June: 'With that clot creating greater and greater pressure on the brain, it is a miracle he didn't suffer a personality change. Ninety per cent of the time he must have felt awful; to have appeared his normal, bubbly self at all is a credit to the unquenchable spirit of the man.'

Michael's death made headline news in all the papers. But the obituary which summed up his personality best and which I think would have pleased him most appeared in the *Daily Telegraph* under the heading 'Gentleman Actor Dies'.

The cremation took place ten days later at Chichester crematorium and was marked by the presence of press, radio, and TV reporters as well as hundreds of members of the public, who I fear had come not so much to mourn Michael as in the hope of catching a glimpse of Liz Taylor, who had flown 7,000 miles in order to be present at the twenty-minute service.

The lawns outside the chapel were massed with floral tributes. But Michael's coffin bore only a single spray of yellow roses with a card which read 'For dearest Michael. Love always, Liz.'

In contrast to the rather brief and bleak funeral ceremony, the memorial service, held at the actors' church, St Paul's, Covent Garden, was more in keeping with Michael's buoyant personality. As many hundreds of mourners streamed into the church they were greeted not with the usual funereal dirge but with a selection of Noel Coward's most popular songs.

The church was packed to capacity and, in addition to the many familiar faces in the front pews, standing at the back were rows of not so familiar faces. Middle-aged ladies, obviously old Wilding fans, wept openly during the service.

Dame Anna Neagle read a personal prayer. Sir Alec Guinness read an amusing but touching little reminder of mortality written by himself, which he called 'Prayer for the Middle-Aged'. Fittingly, it was an actor of a younger generation, Mike and Maggie's close friend Edward Fox, who read the address. After praising Michael's personal courage in the face of illness and personal tragedy, Edward Fox went on to pay tribute to his talents. 'Michael used to put himself down', he declared, 'when he said he had only ever played himself. But those of us in the profession know it is the most difficult thing to do. In his elegance of stage presence and the wit and timing he brought to the difficult art of playing comedy, he had no peer. If the theatre of Sheridan has a true twentieth-century descendant, it was surely brought to us in the person of Michael Wilding.'

As one who was lucky enough to have close contact with Michael during the last year of his life, I never ceased to marvel at the brave face he showed to the world. Many people said that after Maggie's death he lost the will to live. But never once did I see him give way to self-pity, even though it was painfully obvious that his health was deteriorating swiftly. I was often greeted by the sight of a bruised eye or a battered nose, caused by yet another of his falls. But he always laughed at his misfortunes and his sense of fun never deserted him. Time spent in his company was always filled with laughter, so much so that I thought of him as 'the laughing cavalier'.

As for his innermost thoughts, apart from the ever-present sense of loss created by Maggie's death, my guess is they were not altogether sad. On the day we started work on this book, Michael showed me his coat of arms, with the apple tree which – at his suggestion – provided the title. I said to him 'Mike, it must have been quite a daunting challenge to live up to a family that boasts a coat of arms?' He made a wry face and replied 'Alas, I don't think I have added much lustre to the family name.' Then, with his familiar disarming grin, he added 'But taken all in all, you might say I have been a lucky apple.'

The Films of Michael Wilding

Michael Wilding appeared in the following films. In each case the country of origin and the UK release date is given, together with a selective cast list. He also served as stand-in for Douglas Fairbanks junior in *Catherine the Great* (UK, 1934, starring Elisabeth Bergner) and appeared in *Symphony Pastoral* with Mabel Poulton, part of which was filmed in Austria in the 1930s and which was never released.

1933 *Bitter Sweet* (UK) As an extra, with Anna Neagle and Fernand Gravet. Directed by Herbert Wilcox.

1934 *Wild Boy* (UK) As an extra, with Sonnie Hale and Leonora Corbett. Directed by Albert de Courville.

1935 *Late Extra* (UK) With Virginia Cherrill, James Mason, Alastair Sim, Cyril Cusack, Donald Wolfit and Hannen Swaffer. Directed by Albert Parker.

1936 *Wedding Group* (UK) With Fay Compton and Alastair Sim. Directed by Alex Bryce and Campbell Gullan.

1939 *There Ain't No Justice* (UK) With Jimmy Hanley, Edward Rigby, Mary Clare and Phyllis Stanley. Directed by Pen Tennyson.

1940 *Tilly of Bloomsbury* (UK) With Sydney Howard, Jean Gillie, Henry Oscar, Kathleen Harrison, Joy Frankau, Athene Seyler, Michael Denison and Martita Hunt. Directed by Leslie S. Hiscott.

1940 *Convoy* (UK) With Clive Brook, John Clements, Edward Rigby, Mervyn Johns, Stewart Granger, Judy Campbell and Penelope Dudley-Ward. Directed by Pen Tennyson.

1940 *Sailors Don't Care* (UK) With Tom Gamble, Edward Rigby and Jean Gillie. Directed by Oswald Mitchell.

1941 *Sailors Three* (UK) With Tommy Trinder, Claude Hulbert, Carla Lehmann, James Hayter and Jeanne de Casalis. Directed by Walter Forde.

1941 *The Farmer's Wife* (UK) With Basil Sydney, Wilfrid Lawson, Bunty Payne, Patricia Roc, Kenneth Griffith, Nora Swinburne and Edward Rigby. Directed by Norman Lee and Leslie Arliss.

1941 *Spring Meeting* (UK) With Enid Stamp Taylor, Basil Sydney, Sarah Churchill, Nova Pilbeam, W. G. Fay, Margaret Rutherford and Henry Edwards. Directed by Walter C. Mycroft.

1941 *Kipps* (UK) With Michael Redgrave, Diana Wynyard, Arthur Riscoe, Phyllis Calvert, Max Adrian, Edward Rigby, Hermione Baddeley, Frank Pettingell and Peter Graves. Directed by Carol Reed.

1941 *Cottage to Let* (UK) With Leslie Banks, Jeanne de Casalis, Carla Lehmann, Alastair Sim, John Mills and George Cole. Directed by Anthony Asquith.

1942 *Ships with Wings* (UK) With John Clements, Leslie Banks, Jane Baxter, Ann Todd, Basil Sydney, Frank Pettingell, Michael Rennie, Cecil Parker, John Stuart, Hugh Burden and Betty Marsden. Directed by Sergei Nolbandov.

1942 *Secret Mission* (UK) With Hugh Williams, Carla Lehmann, James Mason, Roland Culver, Herbert Lom and Stewart Granger. Directed by Harold French.

1943 *In Which We Serve* (UK) With Noel Coward, John Mills, Bernard Miles, Celia Johnson, Joyce Carey, Kay Walsh, Ballard Berkeley, Kathleen Harrison, Wally Patch, Richard Attenborough, Penelope Dudley-Ward, Kay Young and many others. Directed by Noel Coward and David Lean.

1943 *Undercover* (UK) With John Clements, Tom Walls, Rachel Thomas, Stephen Murray, Mary Morris, Niall MacGinnis and Stanley Baker. Directed by Sergei Nolbandov.

1943 *Dear Octopus* (UK) With Margaret Lockwood, Celia Johnson, Roland Culver, Helen Haye, Athene Seyler, Jean Cadell, Basil Radford, Frederick Leister, Nora Swinburne, Antoinette Cellier, Madge Compton, Irene Handl and many others. Directed by Harold French.

1944 *English Without Tears* (UK) With Penelope Dudley-Ward, Lilli Palmer, Claude Dauphin, Albert Lieven, Roland Culver, Margaret Rutherford, Peggy Cummins, Felix Aylmer, Irene Handl and Esma Cannon. Directed by Harold French.

1946 *Piccadilly Incident* (UK) With Anna Neagle, Frances Mercer, Coral Browne, A. E. Matthews, Edward Rigby and Brenda Bruce. Directed by Herbert Wilcox.

1946 *Carnival* (UK) With Sally Gray, Stanley Holloway, Bernard Miles, Jean Kent, Catherine Lacey, Hazel Court and Brenda Bruce. Directed by Stanley Haynes.

1947 *The Courtneys of Curzon Street* (UK) With Anna Neagle, Gladys Young, Coral Browne, Michael Medwin, Daphne Slater, Jack Watling, Helen Cherry, Bernard Lee and Thora Hird. Directed by Herbert Wilcox.

1948 *An Ideal Husband* (UK) With Paulette Goddard, Hugh Williams, Diana Wynyard, Sir Aubrey Smith, Glynis Johns, Constance Collier and Christine Norden. Directed by Alexander Korda.

1948 *Spring in Park Lane* (UK) With Anna Neagle, Tom Walls, Peter Graves, Marjorie Fielding, Nicholas Phipps, Nigel Patrick and Lana Morris. Directed by Herbert Wilcox.

1949 *Maytime in Mayfair* (UK) With Anna Neagle, Peter Graves, Nicholas Phipps, Thora Hird and Tom Walls. Directed by Herbert Wilcox.

1950 *Under Capricorn* (USA) With Ingrid Bergman, Joseph Cotten, Margaret Leighton, Jack Watling, Cecil Parker and Dennis O'Dea. Directed by Alfred Hitchcock.

1950 *Stage Fright* (UK) With Jane Wyman, Marlene Dietrich, Richard Todd, Alastair Sim, Sybil Thorndike, Kay Walsh, Miles Malleson, Hector MacGregor, Joyce Grenfell, André Morell and Patricia Hitchcock. Directed by Alfred Hitchcock.

1951 *Into the Blue* (UK) With Odile Versois, Jack Hulbert, Constance Cummings and Edward Rigby. Directed by Herbert Wilcox.

1951 *The Law and the Lady* (USA) With Greer Garson, Fernando Lamas and Marjorie Main. Directed by Edwin H. Knopf.

1951 *The Lady with a Lamp* (UK) With Anna Neagle, Gladys Young, Felix Aylmer, Julian D'Albie, Arthur Young, Edwin Styles, Rosalie Crutchley, Peter Graves and Dame Sybil Thorndike. Directed by Herbert Wilcox.

1952 *Derby Day* (UK) With Anna Neagle, Googie Withers, John McCallum, Peter Graves, Gordon Harker, Ralph Reader, Alfie Bass, Nigel Stock, Richard Wattis, Sam Kydd and Raymond Glendenning. Directed by Herbert Wilcox.

1953 *Trent's Last Case* (UK) With Margaret Lockwood, Orson Welles, John McCallum, Miles Malleson, Hugh McDermott, Jack McNaughton and Sam Kydd. Directed by Herbert Wilcox.

1954 *Torch Song* (USA) With Joan Crawford, Gig Young and Marjorie Rambeau. Directed by Charles Walters.

1954 *The Egyptian* (USA) With Jean Simmons, Victor Mature, Gene Tierney, Bella Darvi, Peter Ustinov and Edmund Purdom. Directed by Michael Curtiz.

1955 *The Glass Slipper* (USA) With Leslie Caron, Keenan Wynn, Estelle Winwood and Elsa Lanchester. Directed by Charles Walters.

1956 *The Scarlet Coat* (USA) With Cornel Wilde, George Sanders, Anne Francis and Robert Douglas. Directed by John Sturges.

1956   *Cavalcade* (USA) With Merle Oberon, Marcia Henderson, Caroline Jones and Noel Drayton. Directed by Lewis Allen.

1957   *Zarak* (UK) With Victor Mature, Anita Ekberg, Bonar Colleano, Finlay Currie, Bernard Miles and Eunice Gayson. Directed by Terence Young.

1959   *Danger Within* (UK) With Richard Todd, Bernard Lee, Richard Attenborough, Dennis Price, Donald Houston, William Franklyn, Vincent Ball, Peter Arne, Peter Jones, Terence Alexander and Andrew Faulds. Directed by Don Chaffey.

1960   *Hello London* (UK) With Sonja Henie, Ronnie Graham, Eunice Gayson, Stanley Holloway, Dennis Price, Dora Bryan and Lisa Gastoni. Directed by Sidney Smith.

1960   *The World of Suzie Wong* (UK) With William Holden, Nancy Kwan, Sylvia Syms, Laurence Naismith and Jacqui Chan. Directed by Richard Quine.

1961   *The Naked Edge* (UK) With Gary Cooper, Deborah Kerr, Eric Portman, Diane Cilento, Hermione Gingold and Peter Cushing. Directed by Michael Anderson.

1961   *I Due Nemici* (The Best of Enemies) (Italy) With David Niven, Alberto Sordi, Amedeo Nazzari, Harry Andrews, Noel Harrison, Michael Trubshawe, Bernard Cribbins and Ronald Fraser. Directed by Guy Hamilton.

1963   *A Girl Named Tamiko* (USA) With Laurence Harvey, France Nuyen, Martha Hyer and Gary Merrill. Directed by John Sturges.

1968   *The Sweet Ride* (USA) With Tony Franciosa, Michael Sarrazin, Jacqueline Bisset and Bob Denver. Directed by Harvey Hart.

1970   *Waterloo* (Italy/USSR) With Rod Steiger, Christopher Plummer, Orson Welles, Jack Hawkins, Virginia McKenna, Dan O'Herlihy and Rupert Davies. Directed by Sergei Bondarchuck.

1972   *Lady Caroline Lamb* (Italy/UK) With Sarah Miles, Jon Finch, Richard Chamberlain, John Mills, Margaret Leighton, Pamela Brown, Silvia Monti, Ralph Richardson and Laurence Olivier. Directed by Robert Bolt.

1974   *Frankenstein, The True Story* (USA) With James Mason, Leonard Whiting, David McCallum, Jane Seymour, Nicola Pagett, Michael Sarrazin, Clarissa Kaye, Agnes Moorehead, Margaret Leighton, Sir Ralph Richardson, Sir John Gielgud and Tom Baker. Directed by Jack Smight.

Index